BETWIXT
-AND-
BETWEEN

BETWIXT -AND- BETWEEN:

ESSAYS ON THE WRITING LIFE

JENNY BOULLY

COFFEE HOUSE PRESS
Minneapolis
2018

Coffee House Press books are available to the trade through our primary distributor, Consortium Book Sales & Distribution, cbsd.com or (800) 283-3572. For personal orders, catalogs, or other information, write to info@coffeehousepress.org.

Coffee House Press is a nonprofit literary publishing house. Support from private foundations, corporate giving programs, government programs, and generous individuals helps make the publication of our books possible. We gratefully acknowledge their support in detail in the back of this book.

Library of Congress Cataloging-in-Publication Data

Names: Boully, Jenny, author.
Title: Betwixt-and-between : essays on the writing life / Jenny Boully.
Description: Minneapolis : Coffee House Press, 2018.
Identifiers: LCCN 2017040747 | ISBN 9781566895101 (trade pbk.)
Subjects: LCSH: Authorship.
Classification: LCC PS3602.O89 A6 2018 | DDC 814/.6—dc23
LC record available at https://lccn.loc.gov/2017040747

Printed in the United States of America
25 24 23 22 21 20 19 18   1 2 3 4 5 6 7 8

For Patrick, Penelope, and Augie: *per aspera ad astra*

Contents

Preface

Betwixt-and-between is a phrase that has continually enchanted me ever since I read J. M. Barrie's *The Little White Bird*. Peter Pan is referred to as a "betwixt-and-between"—he is not quite a boy-child nor quite a bird, not wholly living in make-believe nor wholly living in the consequential world. Peter is simultaneously domesticated and feral, devoted and aloof, brave yet vulnerable—I grew attached to such hesitations, refusals, yearnings, oscillating and uncertain desires. It seems to me that my writing life is also a betwixt-and-between, a place where writing that isn't quite *this* or *that* exists, writing that strives or serves to make manifest the inner workings of a life that isn't quite about writing nor quite about living. It is a daydreamy type of life punctuated by pulls of the literary kind—informed by my writing projects and reading but not quite speaking directly to them.

The following essays began to appear when I began to write truly as a writer. The earliest piece was written shortly before I began work on my first book in my early twenties, and the most recent piece was written only recently. Without success, I have tried—despite knowing that they did not, in anyway, fit in—to include some of these in other essay collections. It took me nearly two decades, while writing other books, to realize that I had been writing this very book. What created a motley assemblage when tacked on to other essay collections, suddenly, when arranged together, existed in a way that appeared, in however an in-between state, to cohere.

In revising this work, I tried my best to retain the spirit in which these essays were written; that is, I attempted to make sincere choices and respect the person I was when I wrote them. Some essays showcase my academic inclination, some are more personal, and some live in the realm of imagination. No matter their guises, I hope you will see how multifarious is a writing life, how slowly it grows its pearl, how it is or is not, how it depends on us to call it into being.

Jenny Boully
Evanston, January 2018

BETWIXT
-AND-
BETWEEN

the *future imagined*, the *past imagined*

In the writing life, an occasional glance sometimes out of windows where clouds scuttle and the sky is autumn blue, but somehow one is not a part of it; in the writing life, an occasional glance sometimes into the mirror where the body and one's possessions are caught, but somehow one is not a part of it. I keep meaning to but never do throw the thoughts of the *outside* out. In the writing life, a continual desire to make manifest something known, to somehow be *a part* of it.

Sometimes, I harbor a strange paranoia that although I keep visiting and having visitors to my desk, *nothing* is getting written, but I think that what I do is *write*. I think this because I have fragments all around, and I am sure that I have not written them, yet they keep showing up, and I keep meaning to but never do turn them into something. I refuse to see that the mirror too is glass, a window, a glass with a thin sheet on which I am written, a sheet that keeps the *inside* in. To be a part of it is to be *apart* from it.

How is it that seasons change? Do they change so slowly, so creepingly, because we so rarely break away from whatever it is we are dreaming to notice? What the season brings us to suffer (because seasons, no matter how lovely, will bring us to suffer), it brings when we are not looking. I know the look of a cracked landscape, winter in black and white, flat and finite with a sunset on the horizon like a red heartbeat suffering there. It will take me longer each morning now to go out and face it: the leaves shivering then falling about as if to remind me that somehow, despite leavings, there is some magic, some beauty there. I tell myself I don't want it: the mountain view, the shimmer of summer rain, a trout-filled creek. How is it that I came to be here this way, with the wind a suggestion that it was, *indubitably was,* autumn (already and again)? What I want was in bed; he kissed me and said good-bye. And at three o'clock in the afternoon, the world takes on a stormy look.

Sometimes, I think that maybe I've been on antidepressants and antianxiety medication for the past three years and somehow am not aware of it. I think this because there are medicine bottles all around, stamped with various dates going back three years, and I am sure that I have not been taking any of the pills, but nonetheless, they keep showing up, and I keep meaning to but never do throw them away. I must like to keep them there for the *just in case.*

The present tense is all about immediate feelings, about wanting and lack. The present tense is about things that you don't notice until you can't help but notice them. The present tense is for when you are in your living room crying and the person you love is somehow a part of that, and suddenly there are two possibilities, and the present tense is telling you that you have to choose. The water in the teakettle is boiling. Your tea is ready; either you drink it or you don't.

As a child, I used to love the future tense: *I will be going* and *I am going to.*

With dreaming, we speak differently. We use the past tense. Dreams are about the past, but we want them to be about the present, the future. That is, we will make them *mean* something. I *was* standing over a cliff, looking down on a raging black river. My childhood home drifted in the river. There were no sounds; there was only blackness and stars. Maybe the dream wants to tell me that I have detached myself from something I love; maybe the dream wants to tell me that I will detach myself from something I love. Maybe the dream wants to tell me that despite my wanting otherwise, what I love has detached itself from me, has already begun a journey to make itself live apart from and far from me. What separates me from my childhood home is three hundred yards of falling. To join what I love means to risk dying.

There is a certain kind of daydreaming that can foretell the future. There is a certain kind of daydreaming that only concerns bad futures. In this type of daydreaming, we sink and sink until somehow somewhere inside that dream something loves us again; something or someone says sorry for something that is being talked about in the past tense.

It could happen this way: my mother is still twenty-eight, and she's sewing me dresses and teaching me how to crochet baby blankets for my dolls. If I finish one too soon, she tells me to pull out the yarn and begin again. It could happen this way, being transported back to this very unraveling, and like characters in a movie or story who are jolted out of a quagmire simply by waking, I too will realize that I am not living *here*, that I am still this very small child learning at the hem of her mother. If not a dream, then it could be that my life thus far has merely been an intense daydream. Or perhaps I am presently living a daydream that I dreamed previously. At what point is what I dreamed *mine* and then *not mine*?

At what point are you *mine* and then *not mine*?

This summer, I drove through Wyoming with my father. I had never been to Wyoming, and I certainly never did think I would ever be driving through Wyoming with him; more surreal: it was July, but it was thirty degrees. I was suffering from an attack of shingles, and every once in a while, a bolt of nerve pain would start from my spinal cord and shoot through me. This is all past tense. In the future, I will think back to Wyoming's prairie grass and want to tell others how beautiful it *was,* how the sky, a deep crystal blue, was reflected in puddles within that grass, how the wind, furious and fast, thrashed the grass about until the whole otherwise-bleak landscape became *something else,* something mythical and existing momentarily, hills of sleeping dreams. I remember thinking that I loved my father and wanted to tell him. I told him instead that the sky was so beautiful in the puddles, that the grass looked as if it were alive and full of sparkling stars.

At what point do we let go of the past and enter the present? Wyoming quickly turned into Colorado, and there was a whole other landscape to contend with, a sharper world of peaks and blades, whiteness and grayness, and a sky that was not so deep but a shallow gray-blue. Along the road-sides, there were stones and boulders that once were mountains, which have recanted into another slumber, a slumber that will last for many future years. At what point is a boulder no longer a mountain? And despite the many "Beware of Falling Rocks" signs, I never saw one fall.

At what point are you *mine* and then *not mine*? If I follow you into your dreams, then _____. This is a conditional: if, then. You and I together then, we come together to form separate dreams where something *could occur, might occur, should occur, would occur, could have occurred, might have occurred, should have occurred,* or *would have occurred.*

We call this the conditional tense, although some grammarians do not believe in it, suggesting instead that these conditionals are merely the past or perfect forms of *can, may, shall,* and *will.* But I know the difference; I know they aren't the same. Because the former is about dreaming and the latter is about having, or another form of having. Pregnancy *could occur, might occur, should occur, would occur, could have occurred, might have occurred, should have occurred,* or *would have occurred* vs. *Will* you . . . ? I *will.* You *may,* but choose not to. At what point do our dreams depart? At what point do we stay together regardless?

There are verb tenses in writing that are not taught in schools. These are tenses that one learns instead when one grows older and knows that things will either be or not be, when one finds out that one might have been or might not have been something or other. I will refer to these tenses as the *future imagined* and the *past imagined.*

The future imagined is contingent upon daydreaming, that is, the type of daydreaming that can foretell the future. If I write in the future imagined, you may not know it. Whenever I write my daydreams, I am writing in the future imagined. In this type of daydreaming, the boundary between reality and the imaginary is blurred, and because this type of daydreaming brings the same daydream over and over again, we live out the same moment an endless amount of times, until that moment takes on the same qualities as our memories.

Who is to say that what occurs in my dreams or my day-dreams did not *really* happen to me? If I live them and experience them with the same intensity that I experience events in real life, then who is to say that these dreams or these day-dreams are not real? If you follow me into my dreams, then

_____ .

When we write about dreams, we write them in the *past imagined.* So too do we write in the past imagined when we write about old love affairs, because nothing is as unreal, as dreamy as love. And nothing is as confusing, as cryptic, as encoded as what occurs, as what is said, when we leave a love affair and suddenly have to live again outside of that dream, that dream where something *could occur, might occur, should occur, would occur, could have occurred, might have occurred, should have occurred,* or *would have occurred.*

When does the future imagined become the future? In my future imagined, I am lonely and cold and hunched over a sink washing the few dishes that I have. I have one can of soup. The small apartment is white, and it is winter, and although I am wearing a coat, I am still cold, and my daughter is sleeping in a crib that has been handed down too many times. Not only am I cold and not only is my daughter fatherless, her father doesn't even know about her. In my future imagined, I depart without letting him know because I know he wouldn't want her, wouldn't want this anyhow, so I leave, as ever, with no forwarding address. Not only am I cold and not only is my daughter fatherless and not only does the father not know about my daughter, in my future imagined, I discover that I am dying and I need to find my daughter's father or there will be no one to take care of her. In my future imagined, he has already gone on with his life. When I find him, he is married to a woman with a big nose and bleached hair, and he agrees to take care of my daughter, and I can die as happily as one can die under such circumstances. In my future imagined, there is no apology, no grievances, no *I wish that I had married you instead.* In my future imagined, the only thing that redeems me and the present that sent me plunging into such a future imagined is that he silently thinks to himself, something *could occur, might occur, should occur, would occur, could have occurred, might have occurred, should have occurred,* or *would have occurred.*

When does the future imagined become the future? I have missed my last two periods, and I have developed headaches that doctors can't explain. It doesn't make sense, they say, that the headaches should be on the right side while it is the left side of my face that is going numb. I think maybe the numbness could be residual shingle nerve damage and pain. I mention to the doctors my recent outbreak of shingles, but it doesn't seem to matter to them. The CAT scan has been scheduled for Wednesday. I think of the future imagined, and I can only think that I have, somehow, through my daydreaming, caused a tumor in my brain.

Reasons the chicken pox virus might reactivate: stress, a weakened immune system caused by certain diseases and cancer, taking certain medications, old age. I add to the list: bad dreams, uncertainty, fear, the loss of a baby, heartbreak.

At what point are you *mine* and then *not mine*? When can we trust that the author is using the present or past or future and not the past imagined or future imagined? Once, I had a baby, and I was holding her, and as soon as he showed up, the baby turned into a sheet of paper. Maybe the baby represents what I would really like to have in life, and maybe the sheet of paper represents the writing life; maybe the dream wants to tell me that I can't have one without the other or that I may have one but not the other. Maybe the dream wants to tell me that as long as we are together, I will have to choose; or maybe the dream chooses for me, and thus I will continue to hold a sheet of paper. In the dream, the sheet of paper was unlined and blank. At what point does the living turn into its own memorial? At what point does life transform into words, full of verb tenses, written on sheets of paper? Does the dream decide for us, or do we decide on the dream?

What made the chicken pox virus reactivate in me? I read somewhere that a man who was dying of cancer kept his hope all through chemotherapy and was able to bring his cancer into remission, but then he got a case of shingles that was so bad he wanted to die. The pain from shingles was so much that he killed himself rather than live through it. He was frail, and the shingles had attacked him in the eye. Nerve pain from shingles can last weeks, months, or years after an outbreak; in some cases, it will never go away. Some people say that shingles itch. They never itched me; they burned. They burned and clutched and kept me cramped and bent over. Only when all the scabs had fallen off did I begin to feel an itch, and for months later, there was a phantom itching, a million spiders crawling over my flesh. When does the attack begin and when does it end? For some people, the pain never goes away.

I have a suspicion that in this life, mirrors are not meant for looking *into* but rather for looking *out of;* I only have to master this kind of looking, and then I will be able to see what the *outside* has to offer, instead of only seeing myself looking outward and being confronted with the self who looks outward ad infinitum. Sometimes, I have a paranoia that I am not living this life but another one that was invented for me, and this is only a long daydream, the kind where only bad things happen. But when do the daydreams begin and the dreams end, and where does the sky end and the prairie grass begin? There are stars in the grass. In July, it is thirty degrees. I want to tell my father that I love him. My childhood home goes drifting in the black and raging river. My mother teaches me how to use a needle and thread. To reclaim love is to risk certain death. For some people, the pain from shingles never goes away. The medicine bottles do exhaust themselves despite my not opening them.

At what point are you *mine* and then *not mine*? There are no apologies, no grievances, no *I wish I had*. My mother says that she knows my ailment; she says that in her language, the name of the illness means an explosion of snakebites. Sometimes, I still feel a gripping and then a burning. The test was positive. Then it was negative. My daughter turns into a sheet of paper. I have fragments all around, but they never get turned into anything. In my future imagined, I am dying and this is not conditional. If I had asked my father to stop the car, if I had gone out to look into the puddles of Wyoming sky and prairie-grass stars, would something then *have occurred*? Would I have seen more sky or myself looking to see more sky?

There is a type of daydreaming that can foretell the future, a type of dreaming that explains why nothing is being written. She turns into a sheet of paper. When does the dream stop being a daughter and start being a sheet of paper? At what point are you *mine* and then *not mine*? At what point was she my baby and then not my baby? It was and then it was not. What the season brings us to suffer (because seasons, no matter how lovely, will bring us to suffer), it brings when we are not looking.

I know the look of a cracked landscape, winter in black and white, flat and finite with a sunset on the horizon like a red heartbeat suffering there. It will take me longer each morning now to go out and face it. The CAT scan has been scheduled for Wednesday.

How is it that I came to be here this way, with the wind a suggestion that it was, *indubitably was,* autumn (already and again)? What I want was in bed; he kissed me and said good-bye. And at three o'clock in the afternoon, the world takes on a stormy look.

The X-ray technician asks if there is any possibility I could be pregnant, because if I am, harm to the fetus *could occur, might occur, should occur, would occur, could have occurred, might have occurred, should have occurred,* or *would have occurred.*

Don't move, she says.

For some people, the pain never goes away.

Forecast Essay

Everyone is dying

Everyone is dying. I must remember this always but especially whenever I am on the phone with my mother and she is telling me that her mother has died. I must begin to treat everyone I meet and visit as if they are, very soon, going to die. I too am dying. I need to begin believing this, especially whenever I have a goal of spending the day in my study concentrating on nothing but my writing and do not spend the day in my study writing. I need to begin treating my thoughts, observations, and inclinations, that find themselves manifested as rhythms, that then suggest words and paragraphs and landscapes of syntax, as if they too are dying and will not be remembered again, will never again present themselves with the opportunity to be written down. In order to be a better writer and better reader, I need to believe in my own death and in the death of others.

I will grow into madamhood

Last week, returning my library books, a gentleman passes quickly in front of me, pauses to say, "Excuse me, Miss," before moving on. Today, in the deli, the worker asks, "Can I help you, Miss?" It occurs to me that I am a miss, and I wonder when I will no longer be a miss and will begin to be a ma'am. I am not even quite sure what *ma'am* is; I think it must be an abbreviated version of *madam*. In French, instead of *miss,* there is *mademoiselle,* which means little or young *madame;* therefore, I am a little madam. I will grow into madamhood, just as I grew into miss-hood. A miss is *someone who is addressed.* A girl child is never addressed. (I knew for certain when I ceased to be a girl child, because I was suddenly being addressed.) A madam, on the other hand, *addresses.* I see these women in the deli, and they are not afraid to say what they want before they are addressed. One ma'am in the drug store today even went so far as to address no one in particular, saying loudly, "Hello! We need a cashier here!" while I, a little madam ahead of her in line, waited patiently to pay for my goods. Perhaps madams know that time is, for them, beginning to become compressed, or perhaps time has already gone from them. Perhaps they believe, as misses do not, that they are dying. I will grow from *one who is addressed* into *one who addresses.* Perhaps I should not wait any longer to be addressed; in writing, I should always be the impatient and demanding madam, however premature I think this might be, and address, even if the addressee is no one in particular.

Everything will become so compressed
it will exist no longer

I am wondering where the great libraries are, those libraries that, were they to catch fire, scholars and bibliophiles would be gravely sad, depressed not so much over the loss of the vast amounts of knowledge and history, but rather the loss of books themselves, the binding and stitching and engraving.

The brittle nature of things makes us love them and wish to preserve them. Only when your grandmother is old do you begin to wish that she would live forever. Only when a keepsake begins to show signs of decay or when a beloved sweater begins to fray do we want to treat it more tenderly or perhaps handle it less than we should like.

I am wondering where, in the future, the great libraries will be, as everything is moving toward a state of obliteration. Due to our desire to preserve information in the most compressed form achievable, we may eventually, however inadvertently, erase the very information we are striving to preserve. In my short life, I have seen the compression of the technological means of memory, but I have also witnessed the loss of those memories. Desktop computers have shrunk into ultra-thin laptops; tube televisions have flattened into panel screens; vinyl records have been replaced by compact discs that were then replaced by digital music files; DVDs took the place of VHSs; floppy disks were replaced by tiny memory chips in the bodies of slim computers. I have seen technology break down; I have seen families grieve the loss of their family photos and videos, which were only saved digitally. I have had personal e-mail accounts wiped totally clean by corporations I had entrusted with the preservation of my correspondence. One can only surmise, given the trends of memory compression, that everything will become so compact it will exist no longer; or, the data and information and files will exist, only they will be inaccessible—in other words, they will exist as myth, ghostly, in the realm of the afterlife.

Our drive to keep and preserve seems to have achieved only the obliteration of self and memory. I know someday our technology will have made possible a world that is no longer 3-D; everything will be flat and thin and unperceivable. To live in such a world, humans too will have to transform into beams of light measuring in micro-millimeters. Writers, it seems to me, have been ahead of this technology since the beginning of information storage, as it is they who have always, in efforts to live forever, transferred the whole of their beings onto paper, attempting to take the soul—that very spacious thing—and install it into the finite space of a book.

How writing differs from violent weather

The inhabitants of the earth can do nothing to alter the immediate weather, although they can forecast what the weather might be like. In situations where weather poses an imminent threat to life and shelter, residents, the news stations tell us, should "brace themselves." For a long time, I have known what systems of weather were heading toward me. There were essays churning in the dark overhead, gathering and threatening: an essay on the anatomy of lotus flowers; one concerning the ecology of ponds; treatises on capitalism, slavery, and language; the story of my mother being sold into slavery for bags of rice; the story of my father in cotton fields; a visual essay on celestial bodies; an essay on kelp seahorses. In writing, I want to blend the factual with feeling—not just the speed of wind, the amount of rainfall, the damage of floods, but the emotions of the woman who has just learned that, due to the weather, for which she did or did not brace herself, she has lost everything. To brace myself from the storm of the essay on lotus flowers, I imagine I will have to surround myself with botany illustrations, use nothing but lotus-scented beauty products, visit botanical water gardens, try to remember the taste of the ripe lotus seeds I ate over five summers ago. Perhaps I should not, as residents facing a hurricane, brace myself, but rather take the boards off my windows and let the storm in. Perhaps "bracing" is merely another way of saying "waiting." I should do better to face the storm unprepared and deal with the aftermath—writing that is distraught, malformed, imperfect, ugly, unsuited, soiled, ruined, lost, and irrecoverable— when the storm passes, in those moments when I pretend to but do not really revise anything. How writing then differs from violent weather: in storms you *have not* where once you *had*; in writing you *have* where once you *had not*.

On Writing and Witchcraft

When I was thirteen, I was attracted to witchcraft. I wasn't so much interested in the outcomes of the various spells, but rather I was fascinated by the seemingly arcane and beautiful tools of the craft. It seemed to me that witchcraft was like a really serious spa session, not that I had ever been to a spa. In movies, you see knives and blood, but in the books I stole from bookstores when I was younger, I read about sea salt and candles, catclaw and cowslip, mandrake and lovage, rose hips and wormwood, lavender and thistle.

I knew some kids who really believed they were witches; I also knew some kids who really believed they were vampires. The witches were often suicidal, had the scars to prove it, and didn't appear to have any parents. In biology class, I cut the foot off a frog during a dissection. I let it dry, and when it was dry enough, I pierced it and hung it from a necklace. The witches thought it was a talisman, and they wanted me to give it up. They met me as I was getting off the bus and asked to see it. They went through my necklaces one by one and demanded to know which one was the talisman because, they said, I was not a witch, and I wasn't allowed to have it.

There is a difference between a talisman and an amulet, and although both can be made through witchcraft, my frog's leg was neither a talisman nor an amulet. It was just that: a frog's leg preserved in formaldehyde hanging about my neck. But the witches, who never appeared to go to school and perhaps because of this didn't know how I might acquire a frog's leg, apparently thought that I had captured and killed a frog to make a talisman.

I wanted to begin, initially, by telling you about a textbook representative who came by my office one day. He asked what I taught. I said I taught creative writing. He said his company had many books to help me teach creative writing. He opened his catalog and highlighted many handbooks that were written or edited by important writers. These books would help me teach my students the craft of poetry or the craft of writing, and I suddenly realized that, although I had been forced during my undergraduate education to use such handbooks, I have never used or even considered using such a book in my teaching of writing. I politely feigned interest, holding back my horror and shock that such tools, like medieval medical devices, were used and still being used to teach writing.

Once, I performed a spell to get a boy whom I wasn't in love with to fall in love with me. Unlike most spells in the books, this one only required two ingredients: a pink candle and rose oil. The spell book instructed me to rub the rose oil on the pink candle while envisioning the love this boy and I would share. I was then to burn the candle for three nights, and whenever the candle was burning, I was to keep envisioning this love. I didn't have the rose oil, but I had roses growing outside in my parents' garden; I took the petals and soaked them in water, and I used that water instead. I had many differently colored candles acquired from Wicks 'n' Sticks, a small candle-shop chain located in a mall, where I would also run into and try to evade the witches who thought I had a talisman I should not have.

Perhaps it was because I used rose water instead of rose oil that I had such a terrible time with this boy. He did fall in love with me, and one night, when I refused him, he tried to stab me with a butcher knife. Like many things, I never told my parents about it. I blamed the craft: my motives were insincere; the spell soured.

The witchcraft I read up on was considered white magic. Black magic was dangerous, or so the books said. I read about the terrible things that might happen to you if you performed black magic, usually spells of revenge or spells that would otherwise harm others. To practice black magic was to make a pact with the darkness in the universe. Some books called this darkness the devil. If you practiced black magic, you had to let the wickedness in.

Coincidence or not? When I was twenty-one, I made a pact with myself: my writing should always be sincere.

Although I was horrified by the idea of using a handbook in my writing classes, I thought back to the exercises I was subjected to as an undergraduate. Many of them involved thinking about past situations and then writing through them. In this way, the exercises resembled therapy: confronting an experience with the goal of moving beyond it to free oneself from buried trauma. The writing handbooks seemed to suggest that one could not be a writer if one had bottled up emotions or had not properly dealt with those emotions. Other exercises I remembered had to do with envisioning or making manifest the unknown, giving shape to the unknown. You had to imagine a hypothetical scene and then write through it in order to discover the plot, the drama, the motivations of characters, and, eventually, unlock the ending. In this way, the exercises resembled witchcraft; in witchcraft, you imagine in order to achieve, and it seemed to me that the writing exercises had the identical goal.

Witches are supposed to make an altar in the home. They are to sanctify the altar and keep it sacred by warding off negative feelings and forces. The goal is to purify.

Today, it's eight degrees in Chicago. I left my husband with my in-laws in New York City and returned to Chicago before my teaching semester began so that I could write.

This seems puzzling to others. Why subject myself to a harsh Chicago January when I don't start work again until the end of the month?

In witchcraft, there is something called the threefold law. It means that everything you do has repercussions, and those repercussions will be threefold. So when, with insincerity, I made that boy fall in love with me, I faced, threefold, a very bad repercussion.

I know I'm supposed to be talking about the craft of writers in this essay and not the craft of witches, but I want to do what I'm doing now, and I suppose that this is really what I'm trying to say about writing: it isn't about what you are supposed to do but rather what you want to do, and that is why I have such a hard time with those writing manuals.

So how do I craft? How do I write? It depends on what I am writing. My projects are usually long and considered "book-length," which usually means, at least in the poetry world, more than forty-eight pages. Lewis Carroll said that he believed in "periods of *intense* work followed by periods of *perfect* idleness." I hate to admit that I also operate in this way. I may work on a project for three months and then do nothing for another three months. I wait for the moment; I wait for the conditions to be right. I have to be allowed to be quiet, to mentally hibernate, to clear the clutter in my mind. The more I interact with other people, the more rusty and encumbered I become. In "Levels of Reality in Literature," Italo Calvino writes, "The preliminary condition of any work of literature is that the person who is writing has to invent that first character, who is the author of the work." I find myself spending many months inventing this "I." It is a bit like witchcraft: staging a certain sacredness before the sacredness can start.

When I do get to that sacred place, I work daily there. I make myself write a page a day. I regret that I cannot really speak about craft, that is, about the particulars of fleshing out a sentence or a line or revising it to meet my needs. It may seem absurd to say that a certain mystical dream cloud covers my writing time. The time lasts for about an hour. It begins immediately upon my waking in the morning, and once that cloud has lifted, I find that I can no longer write. I don't force myself, but usually the page has been written before the cloud has lifted.

A talisman will bring things to you, such as power or luck or positive energy or whatever it is you want to come to you, while an amulet will guard and protect you from bad spirits, evil, negative forces, or whatever it is you don't want to come near you.

The writing manuals always remind you to think about the reader, but I find that when I do so, I relinquish sincerity.

The spell sours. The lover whom you made love you will come at you with a knife.

Perhaps, in writing, I leave out a simple fact: that the boy whom I wanted to love me was embedded within the group of witches and was older than me—eighteen—and also a proclaimed Satanist who had carved pentacles and upside-down crosses into his skin. I still do not understand why, at thirteen, I wanted someone who loved the dark to also love me.

In writing, too, there exists the struggle with sincerity and wanting someone to love me. There is a craft in that, I do think: the craft of writing as the craft of getting someone to love me.

I am watching snow blow or else melt into icicles on the various roofs around me. It is twelve degrees. I have no desire to leave my house; I haven't felt like leaving my house in days. I am the happiest I have been in months. I wish for more snow; I wish for a blizzard; I want the blizzard to last for days.

But let's say I'm not writing something very long; let's say that I'm writing a short essay. Then the essay may begin this way: it may begin with a suspicion. I follow that suspicion until it gives me something I might have been searching for. I let it stay that way all day. I get up. I sit down to write again. I see a hole here or there, and I fill it in. I see a connection here or there, and I make the connection or else try to. I rearrange my block paragraphs. I may write from the middle out or pick up from the end again. I let this go on for days sometimes, but rarely more than that, finding that the intensity diminishes after too much sitting.

To prepare for a spell, a witch needs to take a bath in water that has been through some process of purification, which can be done through meditation and sea salt. Depending on the type of spell or ritual to be carried out, certain oils and herbs should be in the bathwater. During the bath, the witch must, in addition to cleansing her body, cleanse her mind. After this, the witch can put on her special robe and chant under the moon that is in a particular phase and throw salt and herbs upon the earth. When I was thirteen, this all sounded like such beautiful fun, but I never had the herbs, and I never was able to cleanse my mind. I made a very bad witch.

When I was in graduate school, there was a boy I thought I was in love with, and this boy told me that I had a dark side he was afraid of and that's why he could not love me.

There are days, like today, when I feel like a very bad writer. I am still terrible at cleansing my mind.

The craft of writing as getting someone to love me despite how dark I might be.

It's difficult to accept that it was twenty years ago when I used to think I could, simply through visualization and the right herbs, get the world to change for me. And that is the worst thing, the thing that clutters my mind the most: there is a *twenty years ago* and the world, despite my deepest wantings, will not change for me. The only thing, really, I can bring to this craft, however dark it is, is to write sincerely because I am dying.

Inner Workings, in Meadows

When I was a child, I often dreamed in meadows. I have never had the occasion to fall asleep and dream in a meadow; rather, my daydreams often were set in meadows. Music happened there; animals gathered, fought, pounced about, lived out their daily dramas to the music that orchestrated in meadows. And, so, I often steered my portable transistor radio in the direction of classical music so that I might imagine animals, fluffy and non-fluffy alike, and relate what it was to live and love and then suffer and die to the melodies and ascents and plummets of violins and concertos. The little piccolo showcased little baby feet sticking in mud, the little buds of growing weeds sending out feelers. The bassoons and cellos came then with a darkness that caused suffering and stole everything away.

I had no knowledge, however, when it came to classical music. I had at that very early age—I don't think I was quite four when I closeted myself with my radio—a desire to play piano. Gingerly, I would pass the electric organ in our living room; the electric organ was there, and I never knew where it had come from, but it was there, and then it wasn't there on account of it having been sold, and so

there was no learning the piano, and there wasn't ever any
fingering of electric organ keys on account of my mother
never letting me. I could not even play on it, never mind
learn to play it properly.

I have always yearned to learn the inner workings of
things; I have always wanted to learn the rules of things.
Growing up, however, I was never afforded opportunities
to do so: I never had a music lesson, a swimming lesson,
a ballet lesson, a painting class. I could never *do* what I
wanted to do.

I take some of this back: in middle school, I asked my father
to purchase a flute that a girl up the street was selling for
fifty dollars so that I could take band so that maybe the
older boy in high school who was in band might notice
me. Although I did learn a little bit about music, that boy
never did notice me, and I never did play well, and the pads
on the used flute were so badly worn that I could never
play well anyway, and the music director asked that I not
attend the concert, where families showed up to hear the
students play at the end of the year, because I did not look
like the other kids and would embarrass him and the other
students, so I did not tell my father, who bought the flute,
about the concert, nor did I attend.

I did not look like the other kids because I was trying to
learn the inner workings of things; I was trying to learn

the inner workings of things without any formal training. My training consisted of listening to music, and the
music explained that there were inner workings and that
emoting properly could release those inner workings so
that others would notice, and at this time I wanted to be
noticed, and so that is why I wrote poetry during home-
room and why I wore my hair the way I did and listened
to the Sugarcubes and imagined that someday someone
would see and understand me. My inner workings would
be laid bare in the meadow.

I would be the animal that, having left the safe confines
of the brushy woods, was suddenly vulnerable to attack,
and so then, on account of that, I would be the animal that
constantly hid in fear. Writing *outside* oftentimes works
like that.

I am the animal that retracts: writing *against* sometimes
works like that. I take another thing back: in high school, I
asked my father if I could attend a class at the city university so that I might take a *real* class, a real *literature* class.
There, I learned that blackness was a ubiquitous octopus
that spit over everything, not just me, and that there were
others who, despite the potential for attack, felt the need
to lay bare for others their inner workings. I wanted to be
an apprentice of the inner workings so that I too could one
day make a great piece that would reveal my inner workings, that is, make me vulnerable to attacks.

It wasn't until I went away to college that I saw a meadow that mirrored the one in my imagination. In that meadow was a barn all enveloped in kudzu; the twilight was a shimmer of corn silk air. There were, however, no animals—at least that I could see—struggling there. So I placed hanging bats in the barn, all dark and slick and shriveled like prunes; they, I imagined, were sick; their babies kept falling from the rafters; their bodies were musical notes orchestrating the air: I gave them a hidden, imagined life there.

Einstein on the Beach/Postmodernism/ Electronic Beeps

On the last day of class this semester, I wanted to give my students the gifts of wonder and inspiration. I wanted them to marvel at things that could be done. For many years now, I have taught and reread Roland Barthes's *Camera Lucida,* and not once during these years (a decade now?) had I stopped to ask my students why Philip Glass and Robert Wilson were photographed by Robert Mapplethorpe. (For Barthes, the young Bobby Wilson is *all* punctum.) On the last day of class, I projected Mapplethorpe's photograph of Glass and Wilson onto the screen.

The photograph has always captured my attention due to its incongruous elements: Wilson's hair is clean-cut, Glass's hair is shaggy; Glass wears white socks and black boots, Wilson wears light sneakers and dark socks. The incongruity is furthered by the visual split in the photograph as well as by the grayer background behind Glass opposite the lighter one behind Wilson. I have never known just where to direct my sight: the entwined limbs, the pointed feet, the commanding hands, the chair backs on the sides of the subjects, Wilson's hard stare, Glass's disheveled hair,

Glass's slight slant toward Wilson, Glass's shoulder in Wilson's space, Wilson's shoe encroaching on Glass's.

I asked my students if they recognized the photograph. Yes, they had seen it in Barthes's book, but not one of them could tell me why the two were photographed together. Then, I tell them that in 1976, the two of them, Glass and Wilson, collaborated on a piece of musical theater called *Einstein on the Beach.* I myself had not heard of *Einstein on the Beach* until I was a graduate student, when I listened to it in my husband's—who was not yet my husband— dorm-style campus apartment, a setting that is, perhaps, in total opposition to the dreamy and enchanting music- scape that is *Einstein on the Beach.* Although I had been, previously that semester, introduced to Schoenberg's twelve-tone method, it had not prepared me for the snow- flakes, the ephemeral sea, the lulling waves crashing that are *Einstein on the Beach.*

I could watch over and over again the PBS documentary *Einstein on the Beach: The Changing Image of Opera,* a film that I showed my students. The film documents the staging of *Einstein on the Beach* in 1984 at the Brooklyn Academy of Music's Next Wave Festival.

And to think, public television used to broadcast such beau- tiful things, I tell them, a statement that makes me realize that I have grown older. I am ever-so-much older than I was in 1976, when *Einstein on the Beach* debuted (and when I was born), and in 1984, when Glass and Wilson put the show on again for the Next Wave Festival, and in 2002, when I heard for the first time, on a CD player, the one-two-three-four-fives.

Einstein on the Beach is an existential electronic pulsing, the pure and perfect postmodernist dream, and like Mapplethorpe's photograph of Wilson and Glass, an arrangement of subtle yet stark incongruity. It riffs from classical dance and opera yet subverts those very traditions at the same time it celebrates them. There is repetition, change through repetition, collaging, splicing of the overheard, fragments of conversations/advertisements/instructions/ trifles, historical inquiry and plundering, the inclusion of the seemingly insignificant and the mundane, a meditative surmounting of the opera's heroic subject.

The background of *Einstein on the Beach* is composed of electronic hums, blips, and beeps; one senses that at its very core is a strange mechanism, an enormous super-computer with no connection to the empirical world nevertheless striving to connect to that world. But I grew up in the '80s. The very soundtrack of my life was electronic. The world pulsed through the sound of electronic machinery. The term *postmodernism* and what it represented was occluded from me; I could not see the forest for the trees. I could fast-forward and rewind, fast-forward and rewind, and hear again and again a phrase or song. I could record my very voice and play it back and speed it up and slow it down again.

I have been thinking about this impulse in my writing; that is, there exists an impulse to false start, to say exact words over again, to abruptly insert a pronouncement, to skip over pertinent parts, to return to a scene over and over again.

I am officially old-fashioned now, now that I can see the forest for the trees.

I do not know how to end this except to say that in video games, which were the playthings of the '80s, when new life was given, it was given with electronic beeping; and when the struggle or flight or fight commenced, there was electronic beeping; and when a death occurred, there was electronic beeping. And I have been hearing these sounds less and less.

On the *Voyager* Golden Records

When I was a child, seeing future dates always made death and old age seem impossible — the future was a thing that was so far away it could never arrive.

With their plutonium stores diminishing, the *Voyager* probes, according to NASA, will be unable to send back information beyond 2025, at best 2030. Perhaps in 1977, when the probes were launched, the year 2025 seemed far off, an unachievable dream; however, now that 2025 is ever-so-near, I still cannot see the present for what it is: even this very year seems unreal, futuristic, beyond what is possible.

That our tether to the *Voyager* probes will sever in 2025 means letting go, forgetting, acknowledging an inability to get in touch ever again. It is more than empirical absence; it is an existential termination.

The *Voyager*'s mission was to chart and analyze our solar system's territory, but its mission was also to go where no probes had gone before. The probes were programed to leave the heliosphere; they would journey on into inter-space and forever remain there, orbiting within our galaxy for billions of years.

In addition to instruments that would analyze and send back data, each probe carried a precious piece of cargo, an identical Golden Record, but other than a stylus, NASA did not send any other technology with which to listen to the audio or reveal the analog images embedded within them.

NASA did, however, equip the records with illustrations of how to decode them, illustrations that would themselves need a fair amount of deciphering. If an alien being were to, in that far-off off-chance, discover the records, it would be faced, first, with the task of interpreting the instructions of how to properly place and time the stylus; from there, it would have to be tech savvy enough to create the analog video images by translating wavelengths in a certain timeframe to a certain number of vertical lines. It seems a nearly impossible task; however, given the effort that went into the planning and implementation of these records, it would seem that the records are more than mere time capsules of how humans will speak to future humans; that is, the records are testimony to how humans wanted to speak to the expanse beyond our solar system, even if that expanse was void of intelligent life.

If a far-off civilization *were* able to decipher the records, it would hear greetings and well-wishes in dozens of Earth languages. In English, it would hear a "Hello from the children of planet Earth." It would hear ocean waves, thunder, wind, a heartbeat, Glenn Gould playing Bach. They would see a nursing infant, snowflakes, a seashell, a musical score, children, a family, a sunset. Morse code would signal a Latin phrase announcing "through hardship to the stars." It is a beautiful sampling, a startling compilation, eerie and ethereal, canonical in its own poetic right. Schoolchildren for all eternity should have to learn what it was that we found precious enough to preserve.

What interests me about the Golden Records, more than their silence and the infinitesimal chance of them being discovered and fully decoded, is that they contain a snapshot of the world—albeit a highly curated one—when I myself was being formed and then born. When the *Voyager* probes were launched in 1977, I was a little over twelve months old.

The records attempt to capture the world as it existed at a particular moment. They speak to who we were as a society and what we valued. We were, in the 1970s, a society that chose to launch what was less a scientific proof and more a sentimental token of our culture's faith in the notions of timelessness and interminable beauty.

Upon discovery of the *Voyager* probes, that hypothetical far-off civilization would also see, but most likely not be able to read, President Jimmy Carter's greeting mounted on each of the spacecrafts that the records are "a present from a small distant world, a token of our sounds, our science, our images, our music, our thoughts, and our feelings," that "we are attempting to survive our time so we may live into yours." To ensure that the records lived into that future, NASA sent the records in thick metal covers meant to protect them from time, interstellar dust, micrometeorite propulsions. The humans who launched the probes understood their own mortality and that the future was indeed a long time in coming.

It will take forty thousand years for the probes to approach the nearest stars they are bound toward. If there exists any life outside of our planet, then it would presumably have to exist near a star such as ours.

If humans have learned anything, they have learned that the preservation and transmittal of knowledge through the ages is a rather difficult and at times futile enterprise, yet it is an endeavor that we pursue nonetheless. Hence the great care when choosing the materials that the records would be composed of; hence the embedded uranium to serve as an atomic clock, measuring time beyond time, so that whatever finds us will know just how long ago it was that we tried. We are a culture that marvels at the survival of artifacts, fortunate that, after four thousand years, the *Epic of Gilgamesh* still lingers here, still speaks.

Forty thousand years is a long time to wait for a chance encounter. Only love should be that foolish. It seems to me that the intended recipient of the *Voyager* Golden Records is a hypothetical addressee, an abstract entity to whom we fling our hope, our love letters, our prayers.

Although I cannot comprehend the infinity of space-time, as the present quickly reaches for 2025, I am grasping, however terrifyingly, the finiteness of a human life. The engineers of the *Voyager* probes are themselves retiring, growing old, passing out of existence, and when they all die, so too will our ability to make sense of the now-crude computer programming language that wrote our way to the stars, the stacks of microfiche with our longing's history, the subtleties of communicating with our vessels that navigate the realms of the in-between and unknown. The data, in other words, will exist, but it will be inaccessible. Deciphering this past will become some future generation's work.

Like the *Voyager* probes, I myself am in my fourth decade; my children are growing up; they will soon be grown and spiral outward until they exist in orbits so far from me; my parents are suffering the sufferings that come with growing older. I know I won't be alive to witness many miraculous deeds of humanity.

Is there any reason to do what we do? To strive to build monuments of remembrance and send them out beyond our lives? I want the *Voyager* Golden Records to be found. But

I wonder why, when I know I won't be alive for such a thing. Why, too, do I carry the hope that a reader will find this essay? Why should I long for my words to have longevity? Perhaps I believe that by building this monument of remembrance I can propel myself into the future and make it so that I truly exist.

I want the records to be found because I, like the humans who launched the *Voyager* probes, am a creature of faith and hope. Perhaps I like to think that if the records are found and deciphered, then the world of 1977 will be resurrected, that I will find myself again encapsulated in a childhood dream, my future still all before me.

The Page as Artifact

If you're spending too much time on the page and not enough time outside the page, then you'll need to find more time to find poetry. The page isn't poetry; rather, the page is poetry's artifact, poetry's afterthought. The page is what happens after the fact.

Poetry happens outside the page. Poetry is an instant. It strikes us oh-so-quickly; it makes us mourn. It happens when life too painfully or too blissfully filters through us. By the time we've acknowledged it, poetry has passed.

That's why we turn then to the page. We want to filter that poetry through the page to give that poetry a place to live again, because it's since stopped living.

The page is artifact to poetry, that is, to what has been.

Can you give to someone else *what has been*? That's the task of the poet. Over six thousand light-years away, almost one thousand years ago, a supernova explosion occurred in the constellation Taurus. When it happened, that was poetry. The Crab Nebula is artifact. We can wonder at its explosion because of that artifact.

Poetry should allow others to wonder at explosions.

Did something explode inside of you? Did something recently die? Is there, today, enough poetry to confront the page?

The line will break; the line will break, and you will need to answer why. Can you answer why? I came upon an answer once, and it was too true; so I stopped with all the line breaking because it frightened me too much. You should know why the line breaks; you should be able to say why. If you don't know why, then you should face each day, not the page, but the break.

Because things will break, and their breaking will make you a poet.

Are you generous enough? Have you enough to give? Or have you lost trust and, as a result, cannot give enough? Sometimes, a poet loses trust. A poet often does not give enough. Giving takes a long time to learn. Giving may not be something that's taught.

When life filters through you, and it has given you a gift (and you've already been gifted as a poet, that is, with the swift ability to conjure language), will you be poet enough to return this gift on the page? Life will filter through you and deposit gifts your way. You must be astute enough to see what each thing has to say.

Poetry is an instant. It is an instant in which transcendence is achieved, where a miracle occurs, and knowledge, experience, and memory are obliterated and transformed into awe. The instant passes quickly, so quickly, and then you are just your regular self again. This instant is what has been; the page is artifact to that.

Is it love that you're after? Immortality? Friendship? Acceptance? Fame? I want to know what your motives are. You should have no motives. Your communion should be wholly sincere.

Sincerity takes time. Sincerity doesn't come easily. The addressee still evades, eludes, escapes you. Is your addressee somewhere enjoying life without you? Or does your addressee flitter somewhere between two clouds? Your prettily packaged artifact: I want to know for whom it is intended.

These things can be learned: rhythm, rhyme, imagery, metaphor, form, synecdoche, line. The tools of the poetry trade are there; they are given easily over to you. But do you know what use there is for metaphor or what form is for? What equivalents exist of these tools in the stars?

So nice of the ancient Greeks to have left us Draco and Scorpius, Cassiopeia and the Pleiades, arrows aimed finitely toward infinity.

They knew that artifice is what we use when dressing the artifact.

The page is where we turn to resuscitate that.

Between Cassiopeia and Perseus

I thought that if I approached late enough, then perhaps it would be sparsely populated and dark enough to allow me to sever a sprig of ivy without having any witnesses. If it grows in a park, then it is public; if a church grows it, then to take it is a sin, although this is not true of sacraments. All summer, I wanted the outdoors in, but the ivy, the other severed flowers, the roots of grasses, and budding potato plants all wizened and wilted, dying from some other original sin.

What causes sadness is living in a different place each August, and each August having fog and rain instead of the Perseid meteor shower. Look toward such and such constellation, and such and such constellation is not there.

Despite the heat wave, what made me want a hot shower was my thinking of Medusa. My last love looked at me and turned to stone. What is feared takes the shape of a serpent. He was afraid, so he had to kill it; while I fear I am not beautiful, and patiently wait and inspect my ivy for roots each morning.

If I have a love story, it exists in the bowl of my breakfast. I don't know how they do it, the ones who drink milk from their bowls when the cereal is all gone.

Every day, something dies: when there is a breeze, it scatters the dead flies on the windowsill; the mouse has been caught; a moth did not find its way out. I think of Elizabeth often, her Man-Moth confusing the moon with a way out. The misprints of the past gather like newspapers waiting to be turned into something else.

For him, I was the only brunette, I know. I was (what is the term for rocket ships that blow up and crash back down to earth?) an anomaly. Not that it matters. There are some weaknesses that reveal themselves only if you wait long enough, that is, if you look diligently for the roots.

I want to know, in the end, what will get set in stone, because what gets set in stone is, of course, final: someone's name, the year of his birth, and the year of her dying—these things unarguably, do not change. I want to know how quickly the quickest of flora grows. As a child, in science class, I remember my teacher saying to take pity on the plants—rooted, they must depend on what is immediately around them to survive and cannot flee those animals that crush or bite. Why is it then that I have feet and yet still refuse to flee?

This place is your private part. When I was eight, Chris lay on top of me and the next day asked for his stuffed duck and toy tugboat back. What is private, what is hidden, should be one's heart, as it becomes more and more difficult to show. All summer, I wanted the outside in; to take that which grows in sacred places is a sin.

August 13 and last year, a bridge in Austin, overcast, high in the upper nineties and zero percent chance of rain. The bats leave the bridge at dusk and return at dawn. The Perseids do not fall here. I think of Elizabeth, of cuttings of newsprint. I don't know why some people want their water so cold, why they ask for ice. It pains my teeth, is so difficult to drink. The way out of an affair is another affair, a misprint for a misprint. I want to know why it is that I have feet and yet still refuse to flee.

Kafka's Garden

January 31. Gardening, hopelessness of the future.
—Kafka, *The Blue Octavo Notebooks*

The string beans embracing the lattice will strive toward some sort of heaven, for in every physical being there exists the imaginings of some spiritual equivalent. If the Beautiful, if the Good do not take root in this life, then they sprout in the life that plants itself directly perpendicular to this one. The lattice for the string beans will serve as some sort of ladder, if not for Jacob, then for the small insects that know nowhere else to go.

It is not so much the gardening that surprises but rather gardening in the dead of an already dead European winter. What I see that F. B. cannot, although she is in perpetual leave, is the frost-formed dew, the minute icicles that cling with blue fingernails to the stiff leaves. What F. B. cannot see that I can is how, weeping, I too cling to something long-since dead.

Instead of the Tree of Life, a silver ash and the poor wren that hobbles there. What of the frozen fruit? If anything is tempting, it is not this, not this garden of grasses that shatters underfoot. Perhaps it is not so much the promise of paradise but rather the promise of *not* paradise that makes me want to uproot radishes, smash the just-buried spring bulbs. A thousand different specimens of lichen have hatched, are roosting upon the stone by the icy gourds. In the mornings, what I see that F. B. does not: myriad red chicks, a splattering rainbow of sitting eggs.

Dreams again of carrots and the red devil claws of rhubarb stalks. Evil must, I know, also have its roots in the garden. I have witnessed the splaying of petals, the curving mounds of earth when new life shies before breaking through. Dreams again of F. B., her white handkerchief fluttering by the frozen fountain, and a snow veiling her visage from me. Evil, I know, must live underground like the badger, the mole, and other animals that take, one by one, those beings I love. Dream of F. B., her frozen mouth, her frozen heart.

It is not the planting that keeps me alive but rather the fear of breaking through the winter ground. How odd that nature too must develop a thick skin in order to survive the cold. Yesterday, a few rocks unearthed and a few potatoes to replace them. Today, a boulder threatens to keep me mad: my shovel impaired, my ungloved hands worked raw. It is not the unearthing that keeps me alive but rather everything that gets substituted, the promise that for every subtraction something living will take its place.

The seed casings remind me of the perplexity of life, how it exists within another perceived life. Come spring, the string beans will, because of my latticing, climb toward infinity; I, possessing the idea of Knowledge, will try through my studies to reach heaven in similar fashion. The perplexity of this life, existing within another life: Hamlet's nutshell and the almond, not eaten, but to be planted to become a tree. What F. B. cannot see that I see: no matter her leavings, we will be united again whether in this life or the next. What I see that F. B. cannot: the ice-covered moss, the rhododendron's hidden fire, the pond iris all ashiver.

Six Black-and-White Movies
in Which I Do Not Find You

1.

Caught in the belly of a whale within a turgid sea and
among me the sorry remains of little fish. There is no color
for blood. (You see, the island will be full of strange fore-
boding.) Even from the inside, I still do not know the struc-
ture of this animal's bones or the location of ambergris. I
do not believe that holding the uvula will save me. Already,
visions of loneliness, somehow drifting ashore to islands,
where I do not find your footprints; already, a yearning for
palm leaves with which to build a little shelter. Among me,
the sorry remains; high up, the spout, through which I
may or may not espy heaven.

2.

This one, a dream: in this movie, they are filming a movie.
The church is one whose bells sound the hours, just down
the street. Autumn again, and whatever looms, looms
large—the passing plane, the overhead crack of poplar
trees, the day all drizzle. I think the director wants to con-
vey a scent of chimney smoke and sin. I keep looking back,
thinking that I have stolen something.

3.

Your farewell attached to my pillow and the curtains are eyelet and the quilted coverlet is eyelet and the pillowcases are eyelet and the bedding is similarly of an eyelet trim; nonetheless, there are no spies outside the window looking in. The dawn comes in like a grave starling.

4.

Sometimes, it just happens like this: the turning of the doorknob suddenly a symbolic event, the shadow becoming the manifestation of impermanence, the soup can a sorry heaving, a suggestion of false fullness. The camera catches whatever sways in the wind: an abandoned swing, the last leaf shaken free from the bare tree, a rope so knotty and veiny that it serves as evidence that the dead indeed rise again. The drawn bath is only an excuse for compassion, a substitute for the letter that does not come. I grow fearful of the mismatched teacups, of the single-serving spoon.

5.

The diner and the lone woman sitting over her coffee have become such a cliché that, considering the summer block-busters, the director decides instead to frame the absence of love in a dog pound. You see, abandonment *does* mean certain death.

6.

This last film is scientific and is being shown on a rickety projector to grade-school kids. The commentator of this film explains that there exists such diversity among organisms, such distances in space that, given evolution and progress, we can never know at any point in space-time the bulk of everything in existence. I love you and fear that astronomical discoveries eclipse me; nevertheless, I keep on morphing and rearranging the scenery. (I alone know that the cause of plate tectonics is humanity's collective yearning, the desire to fit in.) We cannot see atoms, the voice-over insists, yet they exist. If you develop an instrument that is highly sensitive, you can locate almost anything. I am not portrayed as the last survivor of a rare orchid species, nor am I a legendary cowslip possessing miraculous medicinal properties; rather, I am a leaf-cutting ant that, although oblivious to its object at the end of the trail, follows nevertheless with faith that it is being led to *something somewhere*. Then, I am a speckled spot projected onto the ceiling of a planetarium; now a dusty gypsy moth; now as interstellar gas and dust, I am thirteen million light-years away from you. The film concludes by discussing the power of nuclear fission and fusion and then the redemptive promise of reproduction—in the color of lifeless planets, the color of dust: bright pollen, beauteous butterflies.

Moveable Types

Omissions and errors

Before Gutenberg ever thought to carve the alphabet into wooden blocks, he trained in gem cutting. Perhaps it was his lapidary's eye—looking into cut and polished precious stones and discovering inverted pictures of reality—that caused him to imagine the possibilities of mirror images. He carved the reflections of letters and words into wooden blocks and then later, as his father had trained him in metalwork, cast them into metal. In the mid-fifteenth century, he would invent a printing press that utilized moveable type, a system that allowed one to use and then reuse a finite number of text blocks, thus permitting a seemingly infinite arrangement of letters. When the first arrangement of blocks was inked and pressed into paper, it would change forever how we lie. To tell the truth is to be a printing press with non-moveable type; it means to produce thousands of replications of the same message: omissions and errors are the fault of the machinery, not one's own. To admit the truth means to no longer own one's faults but rather to hand them out in pamphlet form.

A warning sign

A warning sign that things will end in a way that will leave
you forever in a state of *missing:* you begin by discussing
books. Inevitably, as the talk of books demands, you will
say, "Oh, really, you haven't read such and such?" and "Oh,
you must!" and "I'll lend you my copy." As one book will lead
to another, and as one author suggests yet another author,
you find yourself in bed again, pressed inside new covers.

A different arrangement of words

Sometimes when I say something, I begin remembering
that someone else has said it before, but maybe with a
different arrangement of words; when I say something in
a particular manner, I begin remembering that someone
has said something in the same way before—only with
me the subject changes. So too whenever I kiss someone
for the first time, I begin remembering someone else who
has kissed me before but in a slightly different way; then
it happens that the only thing that stays is the pressing of
lips; someone else becomes someone else, all kissing in a
way that makes me liken saliva to ink, and this makes me
think that there is no longer any need for speech, everything already having been said before. I think, *I am thinking a thought in the manner of a certain author;* I begin to
think of ways to describe an orange fish by emulating the
style of this author when I remember that my subject is
love; I begin to say, "I love you," but begin instead to talk
about an orange fish.

Never committed to memory

The invention of moveable type can be traced as far back as 1041 in China. Credited to Bi Sheng, who fashioned his blocks of type out of clay, this press possessed over five thousand Chinese characters, which it could manipulate. Given this range of possibility, one must choose carefully when to replace *bat* with *willow leaf,* when to say *open* instead of *downstream,* or when to await *dusk* or *darkening trees.* If the bedroom can be likened to a meta-textual land of signs and symbols, then I should hope to never rely solely on only twenty-six characters with which to move and manipulate, meaning: I only desire one lover, yet I also desire to have infinite possibilities with this lover. Bodies arrange themselves next to one another as if on a printing block, awaiting the turn of the screw, the downward force of a lever to cause the meeting of ink and paper. In the act of lovemaking, two bodies link to form infinite ideograms and phonetic possibilities that are invented only then and never set into type, never committed to memory.

Replication made easy

With replication made easy, one loses the need to commit oneself to memory. The lover with many loves has no need to commit, to treasure over and over again one story among others: it is as easy as visiting one's bookshelf, entering one's library, purchasing titles from one's bookseller, borrowing a book from a friend. With so many possible loves and so little time, one begins to assure one's self that these possible loves *exist somewhere,* will *come sometime* into one's life. There is little panic, therefore, concerning beginnings; there exists much distress over completions. It is easy to begin an affair; it is difficult to tell your lover, "I no longer wish to read you." Frank O'Hara wrote, "It is easy to be beautiful; it is difficult to appear so. I admire you, beloved, for the trap you've set. It's like the final chapter no one reads because the plot is over."

Only two possibilities

In reading and in lovemaking, only two possibilities: *the first time* and *remembering.* The professor envies his students one thing: that this is their first reading of *Tristram Shandy.* The professor admits then to pitying himself and his students one thing: that the book is not being read in its *original:* meaning, the black, blank, and marbled pages are all reproductions of the *idea* of those pages but never the actual pages their significance begs them to be: meaning, *Tristram Shandy* no longer exists, and the only way to prolong its life was to transfer its significance into a simulacrum's life. The used one envies the new one: the new one has yet to come into the rite of her first opening, unveiling; the used one admits then to pitying herself and her lovers one thing: that the book is not being read in its *original:* meaning, it would be lovely to live serially, to await patiently the next chapter instead of acquiring a book completely bound, its ending already fully dressed and departing before the completion of the love act.

The manner in which the cosmos revises

The advent of moveable type meant that the world would slowly become more and more forgiving. If words are not etched and set to be changed nevermore, then mistakes, if discovered, are easily corrected. When someone leaves me too early, I console myself: the cosmos opened a leaflet not meant for me, and departure is the manner in which the cosmos revises. Omissions are often the act of a hand higher than ours; seals set in wax signify that the sender can be tracked; moreover, seals ensure that the enclosed documents or correspondence are *authentic.* To ensure that one remains authentic in the act: never reveal one's signet, never stamp the proof of "I love you." Omit words that find their tongues touching in the darkest and dampest of places; blame it on an oblivious typesetter. The first products of the Gutenberg press were penance pamphlets. Mass reproduction, coupled with the ability to change, produces forgiveness in massive amounts.

A text with endless omissions

In reading and in lovemaking, the memory fails, gives way to self-made omissions. In rereading a book, I have a vague sense of feeling both at home and homesick. What I remember afterwards, I approach again joyfully and, like looking at snapshots of a past trip, nostalgically relive what I lived so wondrously before. What then of all the plot in between I have honestly forgotten? I feel a nausea of panic that I will die soon. I think of (a) all the books I have yet to read, (b) all the books I have read and don't remember clearly or at all, (c) all the books I hope to write, (d) all the books of which I have no knowledge, and (e) the books that may be trying to find me. I think too of how love works, as I have loved many books whose characters, places, plots, and long scenes of ponderings I can't recall, which means, shamefully, that I must be a bad lover. A nausea of panic that I will die soon and the one I love will not remember anything about me other than a few trifling details, such as my name or the memory of a gesture, and that is how I will exist: a text with endless omissions.

Erratum

In an ideal world, we would be able to furnish our lovers, years and years after seeing them last, with an erratum. Although we really mean whatever it is we mean when we say what we say, we realize often, after the fact, that perhaps what we really meant was something else entirely or perhaps we should have said what we said in a slightly different way: perhaps our fates are tied to how we punctuate. My errata: Where I left you with a *semicolon,* I meant *period;* instead of *slay,* please read *stay.* Passages and passages inadvertently omitted will now read, making possible the binding of two mirror-image yet truthful texts: the text of *what is* and the text of *what should have been.*

How to Write on Grand Themes

1. Keep your audience in mind.

As there will always be writing solely for one. It is easy:
imagine that just for once, for you, your beloved begins
to have pity. (He sees how you eye longingly the hands of
the pampered and plush, the groomed young ladies. You
think, *This will never happen; this will never happen to me.*)
For this one and for this one only, you age; your journals
are projected into some lonely future, where, huddled and
cold, you have only one can of soup to last you. The focal
point in the room is the door, through which your beloved
may or may not enter to save you.

2. Include a search for the great unknown.

It may or may not have happened as you had liked, but there
was always something like a chase in it. Over the cliff, you
may or may not have spotted a jewel in the ravine. The boy
with the trembling umbrella may or may not have called
your name. You see, there will be a heavenly castle; there is
a holy grail; there did fall golden apples. The page will always
remain allusive. Give everything then: upon dying, you may
or may not know if he loved you, really loved you—you can
go on, with all of your eye-closing, your convulsing, your
brutal burial, the rites, and the rest of the shrouding and

transporting. You will know then if you were or were not his woman in white.

3. Dream.

It will happen when you least expect it—the mystery explained in terms of what you were feeling. The anonymous letter is not so anonymous, and so you go on addressing, not knowing that all the while there is something in dreams so desperately addressing you. The dove, the wedding gown, the orchid and iris, the precious pillow—you will dream, but you will not have. The monk in white is shaving her hair and eyebrows; the songbird is calling; the fog is not lifting; the traveler will hear voices. Among the rows and rows of cabbages and turnips, only the drifter in sleep will find the one with a heartbeat.

4. (Keep things in.)

(It takes great training to divorce oneself from always-thinking-of-eminent-endings.)

Each morning, you will feel as if you have just done something wrong, as if an apology is in order; however, you will never know to whom your apology should be addressed. It is best, therefore, to keep things in—this way, there will be no exposed skin. He will not know what it was you most wanted; anyhow, he would never have given in.

5. *Pay particular attention to detail.*

Because they will leave you. Every moment, therefore, will be significant. You may not know it in the doing of it, but when he holds you, this is very important. Take note of that sunset. Don't close, do close your eyes. You will wish; it will never happen again. The aforesaid moment already acting as artifact—the teacup so lonely, so empty.

6. *Cry about it.*

But only afterwards. If you lose a child, calm yourself: it was only *imaginary*. She will rise again in her white night-gown; she will ask after her father. Morning sickness will give way to. Always a dull moment; chandeliers shivering. It might be best to be. Incomplete. That is when it might start: the choppy sentences, the fragments, the memory oblique. Beware of the man with a few words. If you lose a child, calm yourself: it was only *virginity*.

7. *Name your enemies.*

You must give up thinking that you will ever be at your best. Blame it on the big capitalistic machine, blame it on the weather, blame it on whatever, but blame you must. Blame it on her, because she was there and she was willing. It was the Sirens' song; it was another strange cacophony of hearts and breaths. You must attribute fault to the fishnet stock-ings, the Brazilian bikini, the manicured nails, the bottle blonde. The devil is real, and she is sleeping with.

Don't allow your readers to know what you are thinking: they are waiting to find faults in your logic, discrepancies in your tone, falters in your dress; they will point out whether you are too young or too old; they will say that your whole wardrobe is nothing more than a gimmick, because they all feel a bit deflated after the harlot's show of skill, her cheap tricks, her sleight of hand.

Hate the pinwheel and glitter. Say his proper name: first name last.

8. Edit lightly.

More often than not, if you are approaching the act of writing due to some internal circumstance, then likely you will not be too attached to whatever it is you are writing. Immediately, you will think that your tone is too self-pitying, too inclusive of the privacy of whatever disaster transpired to you and you alone. No one saw you in the taxi crying. All along, you were giving yourself away too freely; here now is your chance to keep and hold whatever it is you own, to say it and then retract it and say it again and to mean it, to really mean what you say, to *use everything*.

9. Obsess.

Remember: It is not my job, he said. It is not my job to take care of you. Remember: I'll tell you right now, I'll make a terrible. Remember:

10. Invoke the supernatural, especially ghosts.

It will happen, and you will say *chance* or *coincidence*—fate is never something that comes, at least not until much later. (Just when you are thinking that someone may be dying, that person does die.) How else to explain the inner workings? (So fully I believed my sister when she said that inside little perfectly round stones lived the coiled souls of angels.) If you haven't any ghosts now, then invoke them or make them up if *you know who* may or may not be lurking. Say: the mysterious envelope (always too late) is falling from a sublime grace; say: the code matches exactly his license plate; say: the handwriting reminds me of someone I once knew; say: really, I was here before; say: you loved me briefly, but in a lifetime past; say: maybe it was just not meant to be, maybe today I will start calling on fate; say: how did I come to be here in bed with you, and then here again without you?

11. Learn dictation; snap pictures; take good notes.

Never assume that you will remember what is being said when you most need to repeat it to the outside source who may or may not need it more than you do. What is said all needs to be crucial. What is uttered once is just once and all else is but a mere echo. When your lover says, *I love you, I do,* you will want to write it down; you will want to keep rereading it forever. Let us say it this way: the night will not go on, but you will want to keep.

12. *Close quietly.*

Like the rustle of yellowing sycamore leaves; however, if you prefer, the shaking of spring lilies, too, will do. If you want to make a scene, know that your memory will forever be creating one for you. In any event, it will make for a better-written version—all the possibilities and outcomes still intact, with you forever thinking, *Well, what if I had done this or that?* You see, when a lover wants to leave, there is no other outcome. Only when you yourself have left someone will you know what this means—but for now, you are only you, and you are never the one who leaves. It is better to close the theme quietly, with an ever-evasive ending, on tiptoe with breath held, a noose, a sinking stone.

The Art of Fiction

PART 1

Chapter 1

When I first met Butch, he was counting spiders on his ceiling, which he said wasn't the ceiling but rather a metaphor for sky, which itself wasn't a sky at all either but rather a metaphor for *something else,* and so it happened that I fell quite madly in love with Butch; however, Butch never really *happened* either, or maybe he did, but his name was something other than Butch, and the manner in which we'd made the other's acquaintance didn't happen with such significance— but the way I am telling it makes it no different from the telling which occurs quite truthfully under the guise of *fiction,* which means, if it's truly true fiction, which is to say, if it is *true,* then it really is *fiction,* and everything else is a failed mimicry. This takes me back to the ceiling and sky and metaphor and how the ceiling mimicked sky and how sky mimicked how I kept seeing *the sacred* or something like *the sacred* manifesting itself in various guises, and naturally, this led me to loving too completely all types of winged creatures, most specifically luna moths, because they were the most *poetic,* which derives from the Greek *poiesis,* meaning *to make,* meaning one ought to consult Aristotle's *Poetics* right about now and review the relation of poetry to mimicry.

Chapter 2

When I first met Butch, I was in bed alone, staring at my ceiling, counting eyes, which weren't eyes at all but someone who I felt was always with me, who wasn't a person at all but rather a *metaphor.* Butch was standing in a doorway, talking about driving too quickly, driving his truck over a cliff in Paraguay; however, I understood that it wasn't a *truck* or a *cliff* or *Paraguay,* and the doorway meant something I didn't understand just yet.

What the great philosopher says in the span of two sentences, the maladroit novelist takes eight hundred pages to extrapolate. I'm not saying that certain novels are *bad,* I'm only saying that I don't always orgasm, and by *orgasm,* I mean *marginalia* I couldn't help but have. By *marginalia,* I mean the need to underline, to punctuate, to write notes, the characteristic mindful doodling that can only point to one conclusion: that I came across the one golden trail, the one passage in a book that is worth the pages and pages of perfunctory plot and narrative.

I'm not saying that my affair with Butch was *bad;* I'm just saying that I didn't orgasm, and by *orgasm,* I mean *orgasm.* In bed, he was quick and shy, and eyeballs were eyeballs, and spiders were spiders, and the ceiling was a ceiling that never opened up to any heaven.

Chapter 3

When I first met Butch, I was not well-read, and therefore I confused my hermeneutics of suspicion with having brilliant thoughts.

Years later, I became better read: random affairs will do that to you. After a lonely while, I realized that reading smut novels just wasn't my thing: those novels that litter airport terminals and vacation beaches, those novels that are easy to read and end up at some secondhand bookshop that sells nothing but bad sci-fi and horror and romance novels. They are easy; they make the time go by, and maybe you become a bit fond of certain reoccurring characters; however, you realize — after a lonely while — that you need a book that you want to spend the rest of your life with, a book that you can read and reread time and time again and love more and more each time and realize, as the book changes, as books will do, that you change too, and the book loves you back and is a winged thing.

PART 2

Chapter 1

When I first met the father of my daughter, he was not a book I wanted to read because the beginning was so slow and I think he thought I was a sloppy reader anyhow. I'd read a page and put the book away, read a page and put

the book away again, each time reading a bit more until I
realized that I was in love with the book and didn't want to
read it so completely because I didn't want it to end.

What does it mean that the man I am currently in love with
knows more about the literary device of *recognition* than
anyone I know, and looking through my copy of the *Poetics*
for a passage to quote here, I turn randomly to the section
on recognition, which I didn't even know was there?

[This was no accident: my copy of *Aristotle on the Art of
Poetry: With a Supplement on Music* was owned by Nancy
Thorp, who attended Hollins College and who died in an
automobile accident; her parents set up several poetry
awards at the college, one of which I won my sophomore
and senior years; this book was found in the basement of
West, a dormitory at the college, during asbestos removal;
a friend of mine was involved in the cleanup. She spotted
it and thought I should like to have it; I opened it up: on
the front page, in faded blue ink, smudged slightly by a
water stain, read: *Nancy Thorp M. 224.* (I can also guess
that *M.* stands for *Main,* another dormitory on campus, and
that perhaps Nancy lived in Main room 224.) For months,
I thought that perhaps I should try to contact her parents
and send it to them, or maybe donate it to the English
Department or the Hollins Library, but then I realized it
was a winged creature that had somehow found its way to
me for safekeeping.

My digression betrays itself because I wanted to share something, but then I realized that the significance behind the shared object would have to be explained, would take away life from whatever I was meaning to show and tell about previously. Therefore, I had to tell of how I came upon the *Poetics,* and then I felt strongly the urge to tell so much more about my attendance at Hollins, but I realized it had nothing to do with what I was sharing before. I think I can save myself by digging into my *Poetics,* finding the exact quotation regarding *recognition.*]

Chapter 2

When I first met Butch, he was a baby in a bulrush basket, and I held him to my breast to suckle; he didn't especially want it, kept asking me to point the way to Charon. To the ferryman or the moon? I asked before knowing that in these times Pluto is still a god somewhere and not a planet. In this story, my womb is cold and old, and my ovaries sag, deformed like the moons of Pluto. Butch is a baby, and he's in a bulrush basket. I am the way, I say.

In fiction, *digression* means *promise. I promise this will fit in somehow; I'll return to this in a way that will allow sense to be made; the diamond ring is the missing puzzle piece; the jackrabbit gnawing on our celery isn't a diversion from* (as Robert Kelly warns in his book *Doctor of Silence:* beware of animals when they appear in fictions) *what really eats us up when we're in love.* So when the novelist suddenly drops her coveted plot like an expensive vase, beware—love is in the air.

In love, it is easy to forget one's promises to one's self. To be in love means to sleepwalk when the lights are on—to lie wide awake when the lights are out, engaged in some other kind of dreaming. In his essay "Riddled," David Weiss says that love is dangerous behavior. Jeannette Winterson says that those in the most need of change choose to fall in love and then blame it all on fate. To suffer Romeo's woe, professed at the beginning of the play, of no love to bemoan means simply that one has yet to invent a white rabbit.

Chapter 3

In my lying-awake dreams, he has already left me. I don't find out I'm pregnant until a week later. Picking up the phone to call him, I stop myself, and think that because my heart hurts so much, I'd rather do this tragically and, therefore, alone. Years later, he calls me, only because he'd heard, through a mutual acquaintance, that I was dying and that I had a beautiful daughter who had his eyes. I confess that she is his and *Would you like to meet her*? We set up a dinner meeting at my apartment. I dress my daughter in red velvet and ballerina slippers. She eats her peas, plucking them off the plate with her fork. She doesn't speak much, but when she does, he looks at her as if she had wings. I send her to bed promptly after the bread pudding. She is confused by the word *copse* in *Anna*

Karenina; he is impressed, as she is only four. I explain, and she goes back to her room, closing the door behind her. When he leaves, he can hear her footsteps approaching; he kisses her good-bye. Behind the closed door, he over-hears her ask, "Mommy, was that man my daddy?" "No," I say. "You were sent to me in a bulrush basket." All night, she sleeps, and I eat celery in small bites, by the refrigera-tor door, to keep me slightly alive.

PART 3

Chapter 1

What the magicians know will hurt you, as it is they who possess the knowledge of *from whence objects come* and *whither they go.* The white rabbit never exists until sum-moned, and the place where the white rabbit existed before being summoned never existed—only in the spec-tator's mind do these places exist. When the doves fly forth from the magician's breast pocket, they do not enter our world to perch on random branches of earthbound trees—we only see them briefly for the sake of the trick. When I meet whomever it is I meet, this person never existed before and exists then, at the meeting, simply for the sake of the trick. What the magicians know will hurt you, because when whomever it is I meet flies forth from my breast, as they will and as they must, these beings do not enter this world, but go where only the magicians know they belong. Into the black hat of disappearances so many loves go and reemerge as playing cards and the animal manifestations of the symbols of fecundity or hope.

[Digression for the sake of inclusion: One in ten persons aged sixty-five and over has some form of Alzheimer's disease. Nearly half of persons aged eighty-five and over is also affected. There exist chemical agents in these patients' brains that trigger memory loss, and according to researchers, for the Alzheimer's patient, there is no past or future, only the present.]

The need to write fictions arises from the desire to say one thing and mean another. Storytellers are just that: story-tellers. And a lot of storytellers think they are writing fiction; however, the fiction writers, the true writers of fiction, branded with invisible wings, dare not crush the storytellers' egos, dare not dispel their notion of *sky* as *sky.* Fiction writers are wearers of the magician's top hat and like gods, they can create ex nihilo; they spin cocoons around mere storytellers; they emerge as winged things; they begin in various ways; they all say: *When I first met Butch, he was chopping chickens at the block.*

Chapter 2

When I first met Butch, I was already aware that the sky was held together with pins and needles; I had already given up on watercolor, having progressed to charcoal. *You speak in riddles,* he says; no, the riddles sneak into objects, needing the manifestations of ideas. Then a boy blows his horn, hides behind a red wheelbarrow, and cries *wolf.* I mean, someone performed a magic act; I mean, what the red wheelbarrow means is so much more than everything that depends upon it; I mean, *literature.* I mean, give me a bag of bones and I will shake them and cast them into the dirt and make a fiction.

He said he was engaged; he asked, *Do you want me to take her?* She looked up at me and asked, *Mommy, was that man my daddy?* He overheard. She was confused by the word *copse.* A wooded area, I tell her—in this case, where the male characters go, for sport, to shoot birds. *You speak in riddles,* he says.

CONCLUSION

What I mean was, my body wasn't taken with me. When the soul goes, the soul is a very spacious thing. Our dreams were right: we would come to discover, over time, independent yet certain truths. Discovery number one: we will be lonely. Two: no matter what, you will never be privy to my diary. Three: even though the moon may be rising, there will be no weeping trees or intervening ivy, no conscious oaks, no dowagers, no dowries, no contemplating orderlies, no oranges, no redeeming qualities. When you leave, you will leave incredibly softly.

Fragments

The arrangement of words

Every love affair presents itself as a rough draft, to which, ideally, both partners contribute. I wish to delete the last few winters; for the sake of simplicity, I shall refer to this error as X. X and I could not agree on one word in our poem. I wanted *Love;* X insisted on *love*. All winter, X lit fires; all winter, the early mornings were icy and gray, traffic sounded from far away. All winter, in bed, X and I became a hibernating microcosm. X is the embodiment of many persons, all that I have encountered and left behind or was left behind by. The arguments always began in February and continued into April. Once, they ended with a telephone call. While X was conversing, I stole away to the kitchen and sought the use of those refrigerator magnets with words printed on them. I arranged a handful in the manner below and then, having said all I needed to say, departed.

heaving	sky	please	rip	these	delicate	moments

spring will fasten the knife of winter
still I scream to produce a petal
a weak symphony a frantic whisper
we cook a bitter egg and flood language
me aching like the sea

The last thing that X said to me before the phone rang was, "I can't do this forever; something has to give. If you are looking for love with a big *L,* I can't give this to you. I don't know where my heart is. If we continue this way, both of us will succumb to some sort of falsity, which can never be good for a failing love affair. You may know me better than anyone, but it matters little; I am accustomed to being with myself; I stay here alone; I live alone. You can continue sleeping here with me, but no more talk of the future, no more talk of emotion. If you need to say *love,* I prefer you substitute that word with the word *pizza.*"

Somewhere in those last words, if I arrange them to my liking, X said, "I prefer you alone. I give you love with a big *L.* I give you forever; succumb to my heart. Talk of the future, talk of emotion, say *love.* I pizza you."

I resigned myself to knowing that X and I are like two words that do not belong next to one another. If we are two signifiers pointing at the same sign, then we are written in two separate languages; therefore, we may occupy the same story, but we exist in different books, on different bookshelves, in different countries, conjuring our separate connotations.

Lines from the terrible poem

The rough draft exists so that one may partake in ritual: one may rip, crumble, scribble over, cross out, discard, burn, destroy those words that are not arranged to one's liking. The rough draft exists so that one may select those portions that are to one's liking and build on these favorable arrangements.

After confronting an X, after the great deletion, there exists the ritual of ripping the rough draft and attempting to discard it. Afterwards, each morning, drinking tea and mourning, I began thinking about sky. Indeed, I even woke with dreams of sky: the sky a pale blue, blank of clouds, the sky cut here and there by the flight of birds.

One morning, the sky, I remember, existed solely for me. I wrote a poem. It was, like my typical post-breakup heartbreak-without-the-appropriate-mourning-period poems, terrible and forty pages of self-pity, quasi-aubade, quasi-elegy. It took until dawn the next morning to rip the poem to shreds. I drank tea and looked to the sky, which existed exactly as it had the morning before. Taking the poetry shards, I wandered outside and cast them into a cloud of monarchs flitting by. The monarch butterflies carried them away and high into the winds, but a single shard drifted back to me. It said:

depend on the wind
to alter its course, for seasons
to pass, as everything flying
must fall. Just today, the trees began their release

of leaves. It is the way it is between you
and me. I remember you were once in love,
washing our windows in the rain, gazing in

I feel ashamed for having written this, for the emotion, which prompted the writing. I only want to be rid of these lines, to hide them, and all of my life, this fragment will haunt me—me casting it into the wind, the wind returning it. It will get caught in my hair, find its way into my purses and pockets.

When I think of growing older, I am made so happy, consoled, imagining the swarm of paper butterflies that will have accumulated over the years, reminding me perpetually of those things that cannot be so easily discarded.

My consolation

After an occurrence of X, after a great deletion, one which
span stanzas, paragraphs, months, pages, years, I change
location and opt for experiments in form, in hopes of discovering something new, in hopes of discarding the old. If
I am a rough draft of myself, then I am always forgetting; I
am always adding; I am always ripping apart; I am always
confusing, leaving out some important detail, which would
fuse and clear up matters. But, alas, I am a mere rough
draft. Why did X and X and X expect so much?

After deleting one X in particular, I lived in a small cabin
in the coldest place I had ever known. Arranging my books
on the bookshelf, I picked one up that I began but never
finished; on the bookmark, in my handwriting, although I
had forgotten the occasion, was written:

I like to blame all of this on the time of year.

I taped it to the window facing east. Through the blizzards,
it was this fragment that kept me company. And never

did I utter a sound. Never did I see another soul until the spring bulbs were yearning. My writing became sparse, a few words lost in a land of whiteness. Whatever transpires, whatever words arise, whatever is put on the page, it is never my fault, but the weather's; it is always the fault of the weather.

The postcard

Why should I be the one responsible for explanations? X accused me of speaking in cryptic codes and waxing poetic. But why should I waste language, which has never done X and I any good? Why should I waste language, when one sentence says all that needs to be said, says where I've been, who I've seen, what I'm doing, who I'm missing, and who I wish were there? On a postcard, I wrote:

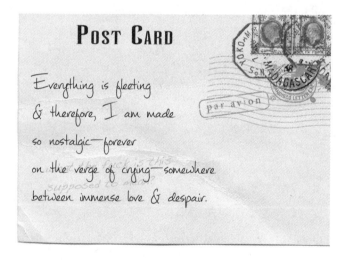

POST CARD

Everything is fleeting & therefore, I am made so nostalgic—forever on the verge of crying—somewhere between immense love & despair.

Two years later, the postcard was returned to me, covered with a multitude of postmarks, some from as far as Japan and Madagascar. Apparently, it had gotten lost all over the world before reaching me. The original inscription was hardly legible; however, I could still make out X's handwriting underneath my own. It said: *What the fuck is this supposed to mean?* Thus, the last words of our relationship; thus, once more, the crossing of oceans and years to reach, once more, the closure of confusion.

The abandoned ones

Some mornings, I attempt beginnings, but that is all. Some mornings, my only consolations are the weather and clouds. I keep trying to make a story arise from whatever transpired between X and me, the big Xs, but there were, along the way, many xs, small xs. These small xs could have been big, but they came at the wrong time, when my plot was still entangled with an X, when my devotion was still focused on an X. And so, I experimented with the small xs to see how they would affect the plot, but they proved to be little more than distractions, and besides, they were so kind, lacked conflict, and promised endings, which were so cliché in their happiness that I, as a rough draft, had to abandon them for the sake of good writing. These small xs clutter my drawers:

x1.

afterwards, she folded her bedsheet like a love letter.

x2.

you have lost your faithful umbrella there.
you have lost your favorite blue shawl.

x3.

i want to love the way birds do—
afterwards, they weave little nests & hush their
chattering cries.

x4.

the creaking uncertainty of the weather-
vane waking you from dreams of falling
horseshoes   blame the summer   the lone cricket
the small, small window

x5.

we will drag this behind
us forever: the slice of blades, the virgining earth,
the loosening sky.

I forget my intentions, but I keep them tucked away, in
the dark, in case I should need them again someday. The
small xs are always waiting; like saints and martyrs, they
will wait until the end, in hope that you will find a way to

use them, somehow, in your draft, but when you do, they will always manage to make you feel guilty for loving them so little, love with a small *l*.

The one I could have done without

I remember, after a long session of revising, struggling, deciding what to keep and what to discard, X made the decision for me: he came over, demanding the return of a hat, dumping a box containing my belongings to the floor. I remember the lilacs and the wisteria and the sky were all purple, and the bumblebees made their way through the crack under my door. The buds on the weeping willows were only beginning to show themselves, and here was X demanding his hat, and I gave it to him even though I wanted to keep it because it smelled faintly of him. And here I was in April, nested in the Blue Ridge Mountains, my most tragic self empathizing with T. S. Eliot, myself transformed into a creature of memory and desire, past and future, my present state nothing more but reflection and longing.

When X left, I looked through the items scattered about the floor: tweezers, a book of matches, a pearl earring missing its backing, my blue bath towel, a few rough drafts, and a scrap of paper, which said:

> people splattered blood on my walls

What a sick-o, I thought, *and all this stuff that I don't need and don't want and have been doing without for so long.* I thought of visiting the butcher for a pint of blood with which to seek my revenge.

The following morning, I watched the fog lift and then the clouds dispersing ever outward and thought that per- haps X hadn't returned the paper scrap out of malice. It was, after all, written in my handwriting; it did, after all, belong to me. I remember later, toward dusk, that I wrote it down sometime in January to remind myself of a disturbing dream I'd had. I can no longer remember the circumstances or persons or place.

22

I remember it beginning this way:

The summer I turned twenty-two was the summer of knives. Shopping always made me nauseated, thinking of all the plastic in the world coupled with the bad fluorescent lighting. *This one is good—for meat and bread*, A. said.

Because it was cheaper, I bought the generic brand of anti-nausea liquid medicine, cherry flavored with a rainbow on the label. At work, I took swigs when no one was looking. It was an art supply store and I wasn't an artist, but I would dream of being able to express myself that way: in water-colors despondent and dripping, in pastels crumbling and mixed with charcoal, in oils thick and embarrassing. I would spend money on brushes, paint, pencils, canvases, but the story never turned out to be the one I wanted to tell myself. The same thing would happen again later, with A.'s guitar.

This must have been about mid-June
because the ennui had set in:

When A. wasn't too heartbroken over some damsel who flocked to some far and foreign locale, he could whip up some interesting recipes. The night of the great fight, he made spinach and pasta. *I can't, I'm nauseated*, I said. What

I didn't know then was that I wasn't feeling nausea but rather the feeling of dying. *A few bites then?* A. asked. *A few bites,* I said. And after, beer and pot and a game of chess. We had no idea what we were doing then, knew no reason to protect ourselves by castling or how to mate with a rook and queen.

Late June:

We found a knife rack at Goodwill, the one where I found the baseball shirt that I so loved. (It was red, and the team was the Braves, and on the back was the number 2; the symbolic significance to me: I would have to learn to be brave on one side even though my heart was longing for union with another on the other.) The first thing A. did when we got home was stick knives into the slits; I never wanted sex again.

This is where the guitar comes in:

I am sick and lonely. A.'s guitar is there, and I can't paint anything, and so I want to make songs. I know no chords, but I can strum and have it sound almost like music. Beth comes over. She's a sexpot, and I know she and A. are still fooling around, but I pretend not to know. She wants me to kiss her. *No,* I say, *I don't want to do that anymore.* I play her my song. She sings, making up the words as we go along: *Somebody stole the kitchen and Boully's oh-so-mad; she's about to lose it, the past and what she had; the bathroom is moldy, the knives are dull; she waits for the milk to curdle; the firecracker wind blows the kitchen to its knees.* Those are the parts I remember: her singing about me and how I could have but I didn't kiss her. She shows me that her bra and panties are leopard print. *I have almost no pubic hair,* she says and lies on my futon.

When A. comes home, Beth and I play our song and he loves it. Beth and I go around everywhere and play our song, and everyone loves it. I tell A. one night when he is sad and dreamy. I tell him, *Beth and I go around everywhere and play our song, and everyone loves it.* He stares at me like a parent. *You are imagining,* he says, *you are imagining this and every-thing to be the way you want it to be, the way you will want it to be when you write about it years from now.*

Because I write this years later and it is June again:

What I didn't know then that I know now is that I kept using the same knife for everything and this pissed A. off to no end. What I didn't know then that I know now is that I wanted A. to love me so that I might love myself. Other things I have since come to realize: (a) those long dusks when A. and I would take mushrooms and stare off into the clouds, forever dispersing outward, and I saw that they were actually drowned women who had been beached, and I felt truly happy, it wasn't that I was truly happy, but instead, truly lost; (b) when Beth told me, you're withering away, what she meant was that I had become the vision of drugged-up, anorexic America; (c) the night I bought

A. the drill and he broke shit up while I made beeswax candles, the night he said he loved me, it wasn't him: his drill and my candles had temporarily possessed him: I know that now.

Horoscope for Cancer, on my birthday—July 8:

Play your cards close to your heart.

This was when July was becoming too hot:

I started caring for the hermit crab because A. had come to resent it. It had a red shell and Beth named it Elgin before giving it to A. as a gift, to get him to "come out of his shell and stop being so damn mean all of the time." I knew it was lonely because it kept burying itself in the sand, and so I got it a companion with a pale green shell. At night, they would touch and talk, and their voices sounded like a violin when someone is new and shy with it. I could never tell Beth and A. how I loved these crabs, how I befriended them and even bathed them and let them roam in the summer grass, how I, like them, would rather be torn apart than lose the security of my shell.

Although I remember summer ending this way,
*   I think this was the last day of July:*

I knew I looked beautiful in Misti's swimsuit, because I was only 108 pounds. I knew this because I weighed myself every day. I knew I looked beautiful because A. and Misti both kept staring at me and debating whether we should skinny-dip. I felt like shit because the night before, A. and I took mushrooms at 1 a.m. and I only got one hour of sleep before getting up for work. While Misti stripped down and A. went over to her, I floated on my back with my ears underwater and stared into the purple sky turning dusk blue. They used to date and lived together for a while before Misti kicked him out because of his temper. I could feel little fish feeding on my feet. Misti swam closer to me, saying, *You know, Jenny, I really want to fuck you — do you ever sweat?*

Sometime in August:

My best friend and college roommate of three years moved into an apartment about ten minutes away. I see her again there. *Where is your Buddha?* she asks. She named my stomach Buddha once when I was high and laughing and rolling about the floor. *Are you eating?* she asks. *Yes,* I say. She says, *I'll be back.* When she returns, she lays a huge German chocolate cake on the table in front of me. *Eat it all,* she says. *I can't,* I say, *I'm nauseated. You're nauseated because you don't eat,* she says. I stare into the cake's coconut flaked icing: a million anemones, waving in the sea, reaching out to me.

Although this should have happened sooner,
  this was toward the end:

All these art books, they say that I need to keep, at all times,
a tube of Payne's Grey. Why Payne's Grey? this sad customer
is asking me. I dream of my answer: *because it is the grey*
of ghosts, like something haunted, a memory mixed with the
blue of dusk to invoke sadness and, as always when there is
sadness in memory, regret; think of every vase you could paint
that way—in Payne's Grey—dreaming of flowers to fill it.

On the EEO Genre Sheet

On interviewing

When I was on the job market, I was asked repeatedly to define *nonfiction*. I knew I could venture into one of two courses: I could give the traditional textbook definition, or I could say what I really felt. If I said what I really felt, then I knew I wouldn't get a campus visit; I wouldn't get the job. If I gave the textbook definition, it would make the interviewers feel that I was on their side, that I was a safe candidate, that I would be someone the chair and dean approved of. Because I have a natural inclination to be rebellious, I always chose to go the road of the untraditional. The interviews then became centered less on my qualifications and more on my transgressions. Some interviewers felt that I was misguided, that I needed counseling, and they would use the space of the interview to do just that. You see, they aimed to tame me, and it became their goal to do that before the next candidate arrived. It wasn't about what I could offer but rather about what they could fix.

On former students

One of my goals as a teacher of nonfiction is to totally destroy every held belief a student has about essays and nonfiction. I expect my students to essay fiercely and obsessively. I want to see, truly, what new thing they will unleash into the universe. One student wrote quite beautifully. She wrote so poetically, but what she wrote wasn't verse. It was essaying; it was essayistic; it was an essay. Many of my students did this over the years, but this one did it quickly and passionately. I met her later, randomly, on a street corner in the West Village. She said that she was depressed; her new teacher wouldn't let her write; her new teacher told her she was writing poetry and the class wasn't a poetry class. She asked her teacher if a prose poem could be nonfiction, and the teacher said no. I told her, why don't you quite discreetly slip her a copy of Pope's "An Essay on Man"?

I kept thinking about my former student and all her talent being crushed by a teacher who could have been in the room interviewing me, asking for my definition of *nonfiction*.

On being mixed

Once, when I was twenty-two, I worked in a mall in Roanoke, Virginia. I worked at several stores in the mall. I needed the money. I could go from part-time shift to part-time shift and not even have to leave the mall. One day, on break, a local came up to me and asked if I was "mixed."

On being mixed 2

So, it seems that I am mixed. I am quite mixed. I am more mixed than many, many people I know. My father grew up knowing only that he was half Cherokee, half white. We've never known where his white ancestors came from; he became a ward of the state when he was eight, and so much of his history was lost. My mother is Thai, but she has curly hair, as do I, which leads me to think there must be something else lurking in there.

In terms of what I write, it seems that my writing is also mixed. I am sometimes called a poet, sometimes an essayist, sometimes a lyric essayist, sometimes a prose poet. My second book was published under the guise of fiction/poetry/essay.

I find these categorizations odd: I have never felt anything other than whole.

It seems to me that the inability to accept a mixed piece of writing is akin to literary discrimination. I think of the Equal Employment Opportunity (EEO) data sheets: choose the genre that you feel most accurately describes you.

Please be X, Y, or Z

I want to know why what is often "other" ends up being labeled as poetry. I think it's equivalent to forcing me to check the ethnicity box on the EEO data sheets. Which ethnicity most accurately describes me? Does this mean to myself or to other people? Other people who meet me for the first time always ask me if I'm Spanish. When they ask me where I'm from, I always say Texas. So that confirms for them that I'm definitely of Hispanic descent. I never say that I am from Thailand. I was born there, but I can't say I'm from there. *From,* to me, denotes a forming of awareness and identity and memory. Most of these happened for me in Texas.

When I was younger and when I dated, my dates were always very uneasy about asking me about my ethnicity. You could see it in their hesitating restaurant decisions, their waiting to see if I'd order in a language other than English if taken to an ethnic restaurant. And then always, inevitably, I'd be asked if I'm Spanish. When I said no, they'd invariably be disappointed. The two most disappointed dates: the Spanish analyst who worked for the government and the boy who had just broken up with his Spanish girlfriend—I don't know what they were hoping to find in me.

Poetry as refuge

A refuge is where unwanted animals go. It is also where some of my submissions to journals end up. Some intern or graduate student has dropped my submission into the poetry pile; in a way, that person has made it possible for my submission to live. It would not have lived in the nonfiction pile. There, it would have starved to death, or it would have been eaten alive. Once, I got a rejection slip from a nonfiction editor saying, "I'm not sure how to take this. I don't know what this is." That particular journal was solely a nonfiction journal; my submission, therefore, had nowhere else to go.

On the EEO genre sheet

I'm not sure which genre I would select. I guess, being who I am and doing the type of work I do, I would have to choose many. Do I choose "other" (if the option is even there) and write in a selection (if there's even a write-in space)? Isn't having to choose, being forced to choose, also essentially an act of bias? Being told that there simply isn't an easy category for you, you just don't fit in, you destroy the natural order of things. The term "other" also immediately connotes an agenda: if you don't fit into one of our predetermined categories, well, you aren't playing the game correctly. You are an other. You will always be an other. You will get thrown into a slush pile marked "origin unknown."

Coda

And so, in the literary world, I find that I spend a lot of time trying to keep everyone from becoming disappointed in me.

I may look like an essay, but I don't act like one. I may look like prose, but I don't speak like it. Or, conversely, I may move like a poem, but I don't look like one.

Do I bend genre? Or does genre bend me? I think it's the latter. I have always been the same person: I have always been made up of three things. My birth may be fictional; I may be from poetry; I might now be living in essays. I cannot see these three things as separate parts of my identity; rather, they form to make one being. I may be the product of fiction, nonfiction, and poetry, but they come together to form one entity. To be told to choose is to be told that you disrupt the neat notion of where things belong, that you don't belong.

The Poet's Education

I don't know if they were monarch butterflies or only butterflies that looked like monarch butterflies, but once a year, when they would descend upon my neighborhood in south San Antonio, I would sneak up on one sucking nectar from one of my family's privet trees and wait for its wings to touch. I would then pluck it between my thumb and forefinger and run inside to my bedroom, where I would let it go, closing the door behind me. I thought they would stay alive forever.

The teachers never knew where to put me. In kindergarten, they put me with the green kids. Then, when they began to see something in me, they moved me to the blue kids. The blue kids had already gone oh-so-far in their studies, and to catch up, I began to fill in my worksheets; the teacher reprimanded me, and I got in trouble for not following directions. This was in kindergarten, when the families in my neighborhood were still mostly white, but not me; no one ever knew about me or what I was or how I fit in. They moved me around a lot back then.

In the children's book *Color My World* by Wayne Carley, the lovely white cat, so fluffy and elegant, escapes its owner's

house to have a pre-nap adventure in a world punctuated
by colors. It rolls itself upon a heap of green, delicate, finger-
like ferns. That was the world in which I wanted to live. I
stole the book from my second-grade classroom.

If you paid fifty cents, you got to see the circus performers
at school or maybe another troop of people doing something entertaining. My sister and I would save our change
so we could attend the shows, and more often than not,
we would have only enough saved for one of us to go. I
remember this circus-themed show so distinctly because
both my sister and I had enough money to go. This was at
school, where we would sometimes, but rarely, also have
the thirty-five cents it cost to eat breakfast. There were
multicolored poodles in the show, and they actually did
jump through hoops.

In third grade, Wayne needed to go to the bathroom really
bad, but Mr. Anvil would not let him. So Wayne, the very
withdrawn and shy and awkward new kid from Hawaii, peed
in his pants, and he grew ever-so-much-more-withdrawn-
and-shy-and-awkward. The class did not laugh at Wayne;
we were all of us very scared for him. Mr. Anvil was overly
strict. He would pound his fist on our foreheads if we forgot
our homework, and he would ask if anyone was at home
in our heads. I did not think any of us, in that classroom,
could be home in our heads. We held our breaths. We cast
glances. We wondered who would be next. I felt so bad for

Wayne; he had asked to go to the bathroom. He must have been so embarrassed and in so much pain.

I wanted to be in the classroom that had a jar of marbles, with one marble given every day for good behavior and a prize attained when the jar was full, but I never had that teacher.

In fourth grade, Mrs. Morgan made me tutor girls in math who were not doing so well. Mostly, they couldn't subtract. I took them to the back table where the ant farms were (ant farms that we made as a class) and tried to teach them simple arithmetic, which they could not understand. I myself did not do this so well. I tried to show them how I did it, by slowly counting out dots or fingers on my hand. I ended up helping them pass by doing all the problems myself and then asking them to add or subtract the number one from another number. Christina in particular was impossible. She kept pointing to Niger on the globe and laughing.

In second grade, I wrote a poem about autumn. It was the first poem I wrote. It had, although I did not know it at the time, a refrain. The refrain was "Fall is the season for all." It was also the season for "going to the mall" and "playing football" and "when the leaves fall."

In fifth grade, Mrs. Lazarus let one of us go outside during fifth period to get the weather report. It was always a

wonderful day for the pupil who went out to get the
weather report, as we were in a school with no windows.
I would note the position of the sun, the cirrus clouds, the
breeze if there was one.

I don't know why all the girls wanted to kill me, but in middle
school, they all suddenly very much wanted to kill me.

I loved a boy really deeply, and I wanted him to know me,
that me inside of me. I listened to the Cure and paid attention to the lyrics, because I felt as if the lyrics were me or
at least could save me, and I knew that I wanted to use
words that way, to save me. I stayed up late on Sunday
nights to watch MTV's *120 Minutes* and to listen to other
words by other bands that might also save me.

Children oftentimes disappeared for weeks, and then they
came back. Or else, they disappeared for years, and then
they came back. Classmates were transient, and the houses
emptied and filled and emptied and filled with new friends
and new classmates. The boy across the street wore the
same orange underwear every day; we knew because we
could see the patch of orange showing through the hole in
the butt of his jeans; he wore the same pair of jeans every
day, and his parents fought often, and his father's car was
sandalwood colored and smoked from the hood, and I felt
bad when I squirted juice from my juice bottle at his jeans

when we were playing because I had forgotten that he wore the same jeans every day and would need to wear them again the next day. He disappeared after that year and never came back.

Josafina came back; she came back although I never did want her to come back because she was one of the girls who wanted to kill me. She wanted to kill me at school and outside of school. When she came back, she had a tattoo on her chest and had changed her name to Sophie. She wanted to kill me, but she would never kill anyone that I knew of. Her brother, however, did. Her brother killed another student at our school and dumped his body in a ditch one block from my house. The helicopters swarmed all morning.

When I was fifteen, I read a poem by Lucille Clifton called "[at last we killed the roaches]," and I thought about my house and all the houses in my neighborhood and all the roaches that maybe I too could kill so as to have a sense of accomplishment and reside in a beautiful world free of roaches.

Because they never did know where to put me, or because certain teachers did not want to deal with me, sometimes I was in *regular* and other times I was in *advanced.* In ninth grade, my English teacher did not let the regular students read the same book that his advanced class was reading, so instead, he made us read *The Heart Is a Lonely Hunter*, and that was the first time I knew that there were others out there, there must have been others out there, just like me, who were sad and lonely and just wanted some kind of beauty in their lives and maybe for a boy to love them.

I was not in advanced English, however, and so I did not get the flyer from the San Antonio Public Library with the guidelines for their Young Pegasus Poetry Award. I saw it on my classmate's desk in advanced biology. I asked him if I could see it, and he said, *Why? Do you actually think you can win?* No, I said, I just want to see it. I wrote down the address and sent in my poems. Later in the summer, I would find out that I did win, and the school would announce it over the intercom, and the school newspaper interviewed me about it, and that boy knew that he did not think I could win and that I had won.

I knew I wanted to write, so I joined journalism in high school. I hated all that late-night work on PageMaker and all that cutting and pasting over the light board. I hated all the phone calling and note taking and blah-blahs of the interviewees, the tedious work of winding film and the shaking of canisters and the smell of the darkroom like pee. Mr. Killough knew I wanted to write more than just news stories, so he let me write the personal column and the feature stories. He said I had to draw the reader in; he said I had to begin with explosions. He taught me how, through writing, I could make something exist that wasn't in the world before.

In my literature book, I would read the poetry section over and over again, always stopping for a long time on Donald Justice's "Poem to Be Read at 3 a.m." I read the poetry section on my own because we were hardly ever assigned poems to read. I would think about who had the light on at 3 a.m. and how that poem was for them and how the poet and the person with the light on were probably both lonely and sad and I was lonely and sad and wanted to have a poem and give one too.

At fifteen, I took an introduction to literature class at the city university. My professor, Steven Kellman, made us read *Heart of Darkness, The Dead, Oedipus Rex, King Lear, The Metamorphosis.* He spoke about symbolism while I doodled flowers into my notebook. I remember him saying always, always saying, *It's as if he's hitting the reader over the head; he's taking a concrete slab and hitting the reader over the head.* The next summer, I took his introduction to film class. We watched *Jules and Jim, Citizen Kane, Rashomon, The Seventh Seal, Wild Strawberries, The Blue Angel, North by Northwest, The Bicycle Thieves.* Those two summers, I felt as if I had left the light on at 3 a.m. and someone had also left it on for me.

When I found out that I could study creative writing in college, it became an obsession of mine to do just that.

I chose Hollins in Roanoke, Virginia. An alum came to interview me in San Antonio. She was interviewing lots of applicants, I think. I didn't know what to wear. She was doing the interviews from an expensive hotel downtown. I didn't know how I would get there. I think my interview went well, because two weeks later, I was invited to campus to compete for a full scholarship, even though I did not have the minimum SAT score to compete for that scholarship. My father put my plane ticket on his credit card. Not knowing better, I didn't pack a dress or anything other than jeans. I prepared nothing. Somehow, I was given a full scholarship, and that's where I went to study poetry. I went to a small all-girls liberal arts school in the South to study literature, physics, and philosophy, and to take a creative writing workshop each and every semester.

When I got to college, I had so much catching up to do. I hadn't ever been taught how to think critically. In high school, our homework consisted of copying answers to questions right out of the book. I didn't know how to come up with my own answers. But I was always a fast learner, and so I learned. I began to tutor the girls in astrophysics, but they could never get it. Brenda was useless; she kept pointing to Gemini and saying, *Oh, look there's Gemini; I'm a Gemini.* But later, she taught me how to cheat on my astronomy lab reports by drawing in the bodies of things that I hadn't even seen.

Freshman year, I took an introduction to creative writing class. My professor gave me a bad grade on my paper on Adrienne Rich's "Diving into the Wreck." She said that it wasn't a wedding poem or about picking up the pieces after a failed marriage and my whole thesis and explication had therefore failed. She said it was about a shipwreck. I said the shipwreck was a metaphor for a personal wreck. Several English degrees later, I can still only read that poem as a poem about a failed marriage. She circled words on my poems and told me that I could never use those words in a poem because they were abstract.

I was an English major, then I chose to double major in English and physics. Then I changed the physics to philosophy my junior year.

When I went home for winter break, I explained Plato's cave allegory to my then-boyfriend. He said, *That's stupid. Why do you want to think about things like that?* I knew then that I'd have to break up with him.

Also during my junior year, I took a course in the eighteenth-century novel, and I read *The Life and Opinions of Tristram Shandy, Gentleman.* That book would change how I thought about books. I had my own reading in class, which my professor would ask me to explicate. It happened mainly because I kept misreading *fortifications* as *fornications,* and partially because I have always had a very dirty mind.

The writer-in-residence during my MA year at Hollins was Brendan Galvin, and he looked us all in the eyes and said, *You better be enough for yourself.* For the rest of my life, I would puzzle over those words, wondering if I interpreted them right, finding that I interpret them differently during different times. At the time, I took comfort in them, but now, they terrify me.

I remember most vividly the lilacs that spring, the spring of my MA year at Hollins. I remember those lilacs more than the lilacs of any spring of my undergraduate years. I also remember most vividly the dogwoods and the dark cuts of midnight blue in the furrows of the Blue Ridge Mountains and the cows on the hills and valleys formed by those mountains. I remember my thesis advisor, Cathryn Hankla, trying to break me of the habit of always using the present perfect progressive tense in my poems, but I didn't want anything to end. I didn't want anything to be *ending.* I remembered everything so exceptionally well that spring because my heart was breaking, and I carried that heartbreak with me for a few more years until I didn't know what else to do with it. It was then that I realized what I wanted more than someone to love were those lilacs, those dogwoods, those curls of wisteria, the fat bumblebees, the air and scenery of southwest Virginia, a place that Kathy

Acker, when she was writer-in-residence my junior year, called heaven on earth.

In Thailand, the summer after I earned my MA, I watched dragonflies and butterflies and birds pair up and mate in the very air. I dipped orchids in holy water and folded myself at the feet of Buddha.

I waited tables while I applied and waited to hear back from MFA programs in poetry. One of my fellow waitresses interrogated me daily about my fake MA. She did research. She wanted to point me out as a fake. I carried drafts of things in my pockets. The cops I served burgers to asked me what good was learning anything if I couldn't help people.

Although I got into my dream school, I didn't accept the offer. I was still feeling sad and didn't feel worthy of getting things that I wanted. So I said no and went to another school instead. There, at the University of Notre Dame, my professor made us study the modernist poets so thoroughly and scan their poems even. It was quite the opposite of what I would have had to do at my dream school. I was oftentimes quite angry. I was working on a book of footnotes, and my resistance to breaking the line was already making everyone quite uneasy.

I moved to New York to follow a boy from Notre Dame, a new boy, a new heart. I had only two hundred dollars, but

I was in the city of my dreams. My roommate made dolls, and she made them talk to her and to each other, and she made me one and told me to keep it in my room. I'd come home some days to find them eating supper or watching TV. Once, there was an invasion of flies. *Jenny, do you think something is rotting?* She began searching behind the fridge and stove. On the counter was her Thanksgiving turkey from a week earlier, where it had sat since Thanksgiving.

I took a course in Dante; I took a course in Ancient Greek. I temped for Avon and Sotheby's and a woman who funded her Village apartment and upstate home on million-dollar grants from a shady nonprofit she was running. I worked as the lowest rung on the ladder in publishing. I began work on my PhD at CUNY's Graduate Center.

Doing my coursework, I tried to fill in gaps that I saw in my poetry education. I studied Victorian and metaphysical poetry. I took literature and arts of the 1850s, fin de siècle literature, and many courses with my dissertation advisor. I wrote a dissertation not on poetry but rather on the entrapment of girl children through enchantment, focusing on J. M. Barrie's Wendy, Lewis Carroll's Alice, Vladimir Nabokov's Lolita, and Henry Darger's Girls.

I tell my students, at the end of the term, that they must have hobbies, because if they don't have hobbies, then that means writing is their hobby, and it shouldn't be that way; writing should be their life and not their hobby. I tell them to learn new things, different things, things that have nothing to do with writing. And not just learn them, but be good at them; master them; impress others with them. What I have learned about great writers: they were always obsessed with something, but they were very seldom obsessed with writing.

Writing Betwixt-and-Between

In J. M. Barrie's *The Little White Bird* (1902), Peter Pan is referred to as a "betwixt-and-between." It is in this book that Peter makes his first appearance in the works of Barrie. We will see him again, each time a bit different, in several more texts. How Barrie delivers the Peter story to us is already, in its nature, hybrid: Peter exists as a beginning in *The Little White Bird,* a play in *Peter Pan* (1904), a new beginning in *Peter Pan in Kensington Gardens* (1906), and finally as a novel in *Peter and Wendy* (1911), which happens to be my favorite.

In all these Peter texts, what I adore is the intermingling of fact and fantasy, real and pretend. Dream-life, death, existence, play, and make-believe all comingle, and one's position in any of these existential states is of grave and serious importance.

In Neverland, death can be performed, but it is also very real. By way of illustration, the narrator of *Peter and Wendy* reminds us that Hook can kill a pirate just to show us, the readers, how easily death is done on the island: poor Skylights hardly lives through the span of a sentence. And so many other deaths abound. Tinker Bell will hardly live for a year, and Wendy Darling, we know, gets too tall to fit

in Peter's world and goes on to have children and grand-
children who Peter replaces her with.

My fascination with *Peter and Wendy* grew out of my fascination with Wendy. She was in love with a betwixt-and-
between who was forgetful, disloyal, and refused to ask her
parents a question on a "very sweet subject." I was in love,
and I too felt as if I were a wee child playing house and
marrying pretend. Because I still felt like a child—I still
do—my love existed in the realm of performance. I played
the good housewife and wanted children to mother. I was
trying to have a baby at the time and could not have a
baby, and so I felt Wendy's want of children and her performance of mother to the Lost Boys most poignantly.

Role-playing and trying on different guises aids in assimi-
lating real life, its successes, its failures, its happenstances
and all. By pretending to be one thing, you can better
accept that you are not another thing.

Perhaps that is where my love for Wendy and for possibility in form began. My book *not merely because of the
unknown that was stalking toward them* is the creative out-
growth of my research on the Peter texts, yes, but it is
also critical theory and a theory on reading insofar as it
suggests, albeit in an experimental way, an alternative to
the traditional academic essay on literary interpretation.
However, it can also be classified as prose poetry because

of *how* it is written, as veiled memoir (I wrote myself into this) and—due to my building on Barrie's story—fiction.

It is also a betwixt-and-between text in *how* it appropriates space. The bisected page, relying on "The Home Under Ground" sections to contain those moments that center on decay, death, and passing out of existence, acts as a casket of sorts, a memento box. The bisected page also interrupts or disrupts the act of reading. So in a text that presents a multiplicity of voices and points of view, there is also a multiplicity of reading experiences.

I could say that my work is not so easily demarcated because its subjects, Peter and Wendy, are also not so easily demarcated, but I find that I often rebel against boundaries, preferring instead to envision, to test, to experiment, to practice, to pretend, to fracture, and then to make anew.

The text could only be subversive; that is, it could only exist as complicated, as yearning, as multifaceted as Wendy Darling—the girl who, as I see it, fell in love with the bad boy, ran away with him, wanted to delight in adult games and desires, to have fantasy cross over into real life.

It could only be its best while playing at its own brand of make-believe. That is, the text is only successful if it truly believes the story it puts forth: that what its author has read between the lines in *Peter and Wendy* is the truer story.

On Beginnings and Endings

To begin is to admit an infatuation, a longing, a love.

A beginning signals that one has moved well past being merely interested and is now immersed in what is most likely an obsession. To begin connotes more than falling in love: to begin is to commit, to stay, to hold.

To write is to encounter a love affair. And as we groom ourselves and struggle to appear our most attractive to our beloveds, so too do we, as writers, want to present ourselves to our readers at our very best.

Or perhaps we get caught unawares: our ragged, disheveled, unsure, untidy, and ugly selves are what make someone else love us, for in writing there is always, inevitably, the ugly.

Love, in writing, is mostly a one-sided love.

Either I love or you love.

And, sometimes—although this is quite rare—we love each other. That is what makes the reader flip the page, that is, read past the beginning.

I am thinking about a beginning that I love, that I adore. I remember, always, so dearly, the beginning of Henry Miller's *Tropic of Cancer:* "I am living in the Villa Borghese." I will always remember "I am living in the Villa Borghese" and the rest of the first page and a half of *Tropic of Cancer.* My teenage marginalia reads, not naively, "This is the most beautiful beginning to a book. Ever." This is something I still believe today. It *is* the most beautiful beginning to a book. Ever.

I adore beginnings.

I adore the beginnings of love affairs.

When I teach a creative writing course, I sometimes photo-copy the first pages of books that I adore. I ask my students to guess the writers, the books. They are often wrong. Not only are they unable to identify a writer or book, they can-not identify the genre.

The uneasy transmission of genre tells me a lot about the nature of love: spontaneous, unplanned, risky, and, yes, that most beautiful of writerly and loverly attributes: suicidal. For to write and to love, and to write and to love sincerely, is to write and to love like a kamikaze.

I loved the GRE Subject Test in Literature because I was asked to match first lines of literature to their authors and books. I, too, often guessed incorrectly, but I enjoyed so deeply the thrill of matchmaking.

However much I love beginnings, I know that eventually, I must write about endings.

I fear endings with the same intensity that I adore beginnings.

The fear is not the opposite, nor the negation, of adoration; it is an altogether different sort of trepidation, for love is nothing if it is not trepidation.

An ending tumbles toward you over and over again; an ending will not stay flat, will not stay put; an ending troubles and taunts; an ending is sleep lost.

An ending is a puzzle without a picture; an ending says that despite whatever it is that one of us wanted, nothing more can be done.

The doctor tells the family of the dying patient: there is nothing more to be done.

An ending tugs and tugs and tugs.

The beginning does not want the ending; the beginning, like so many young people, believes itself to be immortal, trusts the illusory material of existence, and trusts that the distant point in the future that is ever-so-distant will continue to remain ever-so-distant. The ending is composed of distance and illusion; that is why the beginning, having not gone through the middle, believes that it too will live forever.

But we know, despite the feelings a writer possesses upon writing a beginning, that endings happen, that beginnings do indeed come to an end. The book spine betrays; the word count is a demise; each page number a crossing out of calendar days.

An ending is when a leaving leaves.

A beginning is asking: *more please.*

A beginning, in asking for more please, steps into that nebulous, often forgetful, amnesiatic land of the middle.

The middle is the leaving.

The middle is ever-so-full of things that we did together as lovers that matter to no one else but one of us. For the middle is the story of love unrequited.

And so, an ending is when a leaving leaves.

When even the leaving has left you, there still exists ever-so-much white space, an emptiness that tugs you to read the ending once more, to read the beginning again.

An ending says, *I might have loved you once, but things have changed between us; things are different now.* An ending says, *It's not you, it's me.*

Someone has moved on.

Someone has lost his heartbeat.

When I began to write *The Book of Beginnings and Endings,* I felt that beginnings and endings were *true;* that is, the middle was nonsensical: the middle was all but a dream. A beginning stabbed like bright light, sharp stars. An ending lived inside me forever and forever; an ending was played out over and over again until it took on the shape of mourning, and then an ending was mourned until I felt that I could approach a beginning again.

The Book of Beginnings and Endings is just that: it is a book of solely beginnings and endings to hypothetical books. The beginnings end abruptly; the endings begin in the middle of things. It was my book about how love is always only a beginning and an ending.

The middles were only about the despair of the endings: the approaching ending and the ending of beginnings.

The importance of the beginning is to make possible the love affair; the importance of the ending is to make impossible the love affair.

The ending says, *There is nothing else that I can do to keep you, and so—despite the heaviness and the utter heartbreak that you may feel—I leave you with such a small message, such a small sorrow, such a small sound.* That is what an ending should do.

Acknowledgments

I am grateful to the editors of the following publications and anthologies, in which versions of these pieces first appeared:

"the *future imagined,* the *past imagined*" in *MiPOesias*

"Forecast Essay" in *How2*

"On Writing and Witchcraft" in *LUMINA*

"Inner Workings, in Meadows" in *The Force of What's Possible: Writers on Accessibility & the Avant-Garde*

"*Einstein on the Beach*/Postmodernism/Electronic Beeps" in *Essay Daily*

"On the *Voyager* Golden Records" in *Kenyon Review*

"The Page as Artifact" in *Poets on Teaching: A Sourcebook*

"Between Cassiopeia and Perseus" in *DIAGRAM*

"Kafka's Garden" in *Unsaid*

"Six Black-and-White Movies in Which I Do Not Find You" in *Tarpaulin Sky*

"Moveable Types" in *Maisonneuve*

"How to Write on Grand Themes" in *MiPOesias*

"The Art of Fiction" in *ArielX*

"Fragments" in *Another Chicago Magazine* and *effing magazine*

"22" in *Coconut*

"On the EEO Genre Sheet" in *Bending Genre: Essays on Creative Nonfiction*

"Writing Betwixt-and-Between" in *Family Resemblance: An Anthology and Exploration of Eight Hybrid Literary Genres*

"On Beginnings and Endings" in *The Rose Metal Press Field Guide to Writing Flash Nonfiction*

"The Poet's Education" was a talk given for the Chicago Poetry Project's "Poets Talking" lecture series.

Additionally, the following essays also appeared in the now out-of-print chapbook *Moveable Types:* "Forecast Essay," "Kafka's Garden," "Moveable Types," "Fragments," and "22." "22," "Fragments," and "Between Cassiopeia and Perseus" also appeared in *of the mismatched teacups, of the single-serving spoon: a book of failures.*

I also wish to express my extreme gratitude to Coffee House Press, especially to Chris Fischbach, who quickly believed in this book; to Caroline Casey, who knew there was something there; and, most importantly, to Carla Valadez, who, through her meticulous reading and devotion to *meaning,* made me believe in this book too.

LITERATURE
is not the same thing as
PUBLISHING

Coffee House Press began as a small letterpress operation in 1972 and has grown into an internationally renowned nonprofit publisher of literary fiction, essay, poetry, and other work that doesn't fit neatly into genre categories.

Coffee House is both a publisher and an arts organization. Through our *Books in Action* program and publications, we've become inter-disciplinary collaborators and incubators for new work and audience experiences. Our vision for the future is one where a publisher is a catalyst and connector.

Funder Acknowledgments

Coffee House Press is an internationally renowned independent book publisher and arts nonprofit based in Minneapolis, MN; through its literary publications and *Books in Action* program, Coffee House acts as a catalyst and connector—between authors and readers, ideas and resources, creativity and community, inspiration and action.

Coffee House Press books are made possible through the generous support of grants and donations from corporations, state and federal grant programs, family foundations, and the many individuals who believe in the transformational power of literature. This activity is made possible by the voters of Minnesota through a Minnesota State Arts Board Operating Support grant, thanks to the legislative appropriation from the arts and cultural heritage fund. Coffee House also receives major operating support from the Amazon Literary Partnership, the Jerome Foundation, The McKnight Foundation, Target Foundation, and the National Endowment for the Arts (NEA). To find out more about how NEA grants impact individuals and communities, visit www.arts.gov.

Coffee House Press receives additional support from the Elmer L. & Eleanor J. Andersen Foundation; the David & Mary Anderson Family Foundation; the Buuck Family Foundation; Fredrikson & Byron, P.A.; Dorsey & Whitney LLP; the Fringe Foundation; Kenneth Koch Literary Estate; the Knight Foundation; the Rehael Fund of the Minneapolis Foundation; the Matching Grant Program Fund of the Minneapolis Foundation; Mr. Pancks' Fund in memory of Graham Kimpton; the Schwab Charitable Fund; Schwegman, Lundberg & Woessner, P.A.; the U.S. Bank Foundation; VSA Minnesota for the Metropolitan Regional Arts Council; and the Woessner Freeman Family Foundation in honor of Allan Kornblum.

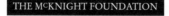

The Publisher's Circle of Coffee House Press

Publisher's Circle members make significant contributions to Coffee House Press's annual giving campaign. Understanding that a strong financial base is necessary for the press to meet the challenges and opportunities that arise each year, this group plays a crucial part in the success of Coffee House's mission.

Recent Publisher's Circle members include many anonymous donors, Suzanne Allen, Patricia A. Beithon, the E. Thomas Binger & Rebecca Rand Fund of the Minneapolis Foundation, Robert & Gail Buuck, Claire Casey, Louise Copeland, Jane Dalrymple-Hollo, Mary Ebert & Paul Stembler, Kaywin Feldman & Jim Lutz, Chris Fischbach & Katie Dublinski, Sally French, Jocelyn Hale & Glenn Miller, the Rehael Fund-Roger Hale/Nor Hall of the Minneapolis Foundation, Randy Hartten & Ron Lotz, Dylan Hicks & Nina Hale, William Hardacker, Jeffrey Hom, Carl & Heidi Horsch, Amy L. Hubbard & Geoffrey J. Kehoe Fund, Kenneth Kahn & Susan Dicker, Stephen & Isabel Keating, Kenneth Koch Literary Estate, Cinda Kornblum, Jennifer Kwon Dobbs & Stefan Liess, Lenfestey Family Foundation, Sarah Lutman & Rob Rudolph, the Carol & Aaron Mack Charitable Fund of the Minneapolis Foundation, George & Olga Mack, Joshua Mack & Ron Warren, Gillian McCain, Mary & Malcolm McDermid, Sjur Midness & Briar Andresen, Maureen Millea Smith & Daniel Smith, Peter Nelson & Jennifer Swenson, Enrique & Jennifer Olivarez, Alan Polsky, Marc Porter & James Hennessy, Robin Preble, Alexis Scott, Ruth Stricker Dayton, Jeffrey Sugerman & Sarah Schultz, Nan G. & Stephen C. Swid, Patricia Tilton, Joanne Von Blon, Stu Wilson & Melissa Barker, Warren D. Woessner & Iris C. Freeman, Margaret Wurtele, and Wayne P. Zink & Christopher Schout.

For more information about the Publisher's Circle and other ways to support Coffee House Press books, authors, and activities, please visit www.coffeehousepress.org/support or contact us at info@coffeehousepress.org.

Essays on Writing from Coffee House Press

How We Speak to One Another:
An Essay Daily Reader

edited by Ander Monson
and Craig Reinbold

The Deep Zoo
by Rikki Ducornet

JENNY BOULLY is the author of *The Body, The Book of Beginnings and Endings, not merely because of the unknown that was stalking toward them,* and other books. Born in Thailand, she grew up in Texas and holds a PhD in English from the Graduate Center of the City University of New York. She teaches creative writing and literature at Columbia College Chicago.

Betwixt-and-Between was designed by
Bookmobile Design & Digital Publisher Services.
Text is set in Anziano.